Dr. D. James Kennedy—a man with an idea that will count for eternity.

"I can enthusiastically recommend the Coral Ridge Evangelism Program that Dr. D. James Kennedy taught us as the answer to the spiritual growth in our church."

—REVEREND ROBERT F. ARMSTRONG
Warrendale Community Church
Number One Sunday School (1970)
Class A Division,
National Sunday School Association

"One of the most exciting days of my life was the first time I went out and shared with a friend who Jesus Christ really is and how you could know for certain that you are going to Heaven."

—DOTTIE SPRINGER, LAY EVANGELIST
Coral Ridge Presbyterian Church

"A little over two years have passed since our first contact with your program, and I think I'm safe in saying that more practical evangelism has been taking place in Michigan during these two years than in the total eighty-nine-year history of our District."

—REVEREND GERALD SCHULTZ
Detroit, Michigan

BORN IN SUNNY LOS ANGELES, CALIFORNIA, while it still was, author E. Russell Chandler allowed himself to be transplanted into busy Washington, D.C., where he is News Editor for *Christianity Today* magazine.

A speaker, writer, editor, former pastor, "Russ," as he is called by his friends, is a member of the National Press Club, the White House Correspondents Association, and the Religion Newswriters Association.

Russ, his wife Sandra, and their three children Heather, Holly, and Timothy live in Alexandria, Virginia.

His skills as a writer and editor become readily apparent as you read Russ' informative story of Dr. D. James Kennedy. Russ' analysis of the man gleaned from hours of interview with Dr. Kennedy in person and through tapes, writings, and conversations; his picturesque style of writing about interviews with people; his ability to make history live combine to make this book a truly enjoyable reading experience.

The story of Dr. D. James Kennedy
and the astonishing things that happen when
laymen learn to share their faith.

The Kennedy Explosion

*by E. Russell
Chandler*

DAVID C. COOK PUBLISHING CO.

Elgin, IL 60120

THE KENNEDY EXPLOSION

The story of Dr. D. James Kennedy and the astonishing things that happen when laymen learn to share their faith.

Published for the David C. Cook Publishing Co. by Keats Publishing, Inc.

Second printing, May, 1972

Library of Congress Catalog Card Number: 79-178886
ISBN: 0-912692-02-2
Printed in the United States of America

To my new friends in the Lord at Coral Ridge; my wife and partner, Sandie; and my beloved children, Heather, Holly, and Timothy, whose help and patience made this book possible.

"There is one thing stronger than all the armies in the world; and that is an idea whose time has come."

—ASCRIBED TO VICTOR HUGO

(paraphrase of Historie d'un Crime; Conclusion: "La Chute," chapter 10, page 649.)

Contents

1: DANCING IN THE PULPIT

A handsome, dark-haired college dropout was making $300 a week as manager of the Tampa, Florida, Arthur Murray dance studio. That is, until he became suddenly unemployed at 6:00 P. M. Saturday, December 3, 1955.

At 11:30 the next morning he was preaching his first sermon—ever—from the pulpit of a tiny Presbyterian church in Clearwater. As its pastor!

It was hard to tell who was the more surprised, the fledgling preacher or the congregation. The former pastor had just unexpectedly told his parishioners that the nervous young man was their new minister.

"Now that just doesn't happen very often, let me tell you," recalls D. James Kennedy.

But things have not happened in the usual way for the Reverend James Kennedy, now the pastor of one of America's fastest-growing churches and leader of a unique evangelism program sweeping the nation, racing across Canada like prairie fire—and spreading overseas into dozens of countries.

Ever since he accepted God's free gift of eternal life, Kennedy has laid it on the line for Jesus Christ. A strapping six-footer with a rugged mien, a firm hand shake, and a ready smile, Jim Kennedy won't compromise his vision to reach for Christ everyone, everywhere, in every way possible, in this generation.

In the beginning he stoutly resisted the call to the ministry. As long as he could, that is.

Jim Kennedy attended a Presbyterian church in Tampa after his conversion and while he was employed at the Murray studio. One day after the service, a dignified lady with a mink stole approached Kennedy—a new Christian—and breathed authoritatively: "You know, you ought to be in the ministry."

Jim laughed.

But God began to use her words to convict Jim's heart.

A struggle began. Basically, Jim didn't want to give up the money—sometimes up to $700 a week—he was making at the studio. Not bad money for a single, swinging guy in his early twenties, in 1955.

There were other little pressures as well. Jim had "sold" $500 worth of dancing lessons to a pretty young brunette named Anne Lewis, and he had a follow-up matrimonial pitch all planned.

Anne's sister had married a minister. Anne had reacted negatively. "I'll *never* marry a minister," she had already told Jim flatly, the thought never occurring to her that he might ever become one.

Then there was the man at the Christian Business Men's Club who badgered Jim about being a member of the CBMC deputation team on Sunday nights and waltzing girls around a dance studio the rest of the week.

"How can you give a convincing testimony and work

12

in a place like *that*?" jabbed his accuser one night.

Jim was furious!

Tormented, he went back to his studio office, locked the door—and got down on his knees:

"Lord, if You don't want me here I'll quit. Unless You make it plain You do want me here, in fact, I'll quit. Unless You make it plain You want me here, I'm going to call up the studio owner in Miami and tell him that I'm quitting. Right now."

Jim started dialing. Then he stopped! He cradled the phone and again dropped to his knees: "If You *really* want me to do this—unless You do something— I'm going to quit."

Pause. Silence.

"Lord, who needs a second-hand Christian mambo dancer? . . . But I don't know how to do anything else," Jim prayed a third time.

Then he put through the call.

"I was just going to call *you*," greeted the voice on the other end of the line. "How would you like to run the Sarasota studio—with a half-interest in its owner-ship?"

Satan was tempting! Jim had discovered only that day that—despite his good earnings—his bank account had shriveled to a mere $13.

"Umm, I called to tell you I'm going to . . . ah . . . quit," Jim faltered.

The Miami man coaxed and pleaded. But when it became apparent Jim wasn't budging, the owner grew petulant: "Well, if that's how it is, I'll have your replacement by Sunday!"

Jim hung up! Afraid he had ruined his life, he turned to his pastor, at the church where he had taught Bible classes, for advice and help.

"There's this home mission church, Bethel, in Clearwater. You can preach there Sunday," the pastor offered. "They might be in need of a supply preacher soon. The old minister who's filling in is planning to retire next February—maybe."

I'm going to be the skinniest preacher they ever had by that time, thought Jim.

Jim, and Anne, whom he was dating at the time, arrived at the old, rundown, white stone church in Clearwater the next morning—the first Sunday morning in December, 1955. They were awed by the elderly supply preacher, formal and august in his flowing robes.

Jim had prepared a sermon (his first, though he had taught Bible classes) on the wedding garment in the marriage feast (Matthew 22: 11-14). His throat was dry and his hands perspired as he sat on the platform while the gowned pastor handled the first part of the service. Then came announcements.

"Well, now, the home missions committee has sent over this young man," the pastor began. "I've been thinking of retiring for some time. I've just decided I'm going to retire now. Here's your new preacher."

The congregation, of course, had no say in the matter. Nor had the shy dance instructor who admits he was "scared to death."

Jim was so nervous, in fact, that when he stepped into the pulpit to deliver the sermon, he started shifting from one foot back to the other as he spoke.

"I was doing things with my feet I wasn't even aware of," Kennedy chuckles. "I was actually dancing in the pulpit!"

The old pastor was sitting behind him. His eyes popped. He had just given this young man to the church!

Anne later told Jim that the pastor looked at Jim in astonishment—and the congregation watched him watch. Nobody paid much attention to the sermon.

God and fast footwork took Jim from Arthur Murray to the pulpit of Bethel church in Clearwater.

2: AN INESCAPABLE QUESTION

Greater things lay ahead for God's second-hand mambo dancer, but let us pause in our story to flash back briefly for a vital episode in the Kennedy story.

At 2 P. M. one quiet Sunday afternoon the clock radio shattered the stillness of Jim Kennedy's small Tampa apartment. A radio preacher came on strongly.

Groggily, Jim stumbled out of bed and fumbled for the radio dial. He had been at a studio [Arthur Murray] party at a local hotel until 4:00 that morning. Ordinarily he went to work about 1:00, but today was Sunday and he was sleeping in.

He reached for the dial to switch to some music. Before he could turn the knob, though, the Presbyterian minister stopped him cold with a startling question:

"Suppose that you were to die tonight and stand before God and He were to say to you, 'Why should I let you into My Heaven?' what would you say?"

The speaker was the late Dr. Donald Grey Barnhouse, pastor of Philadelphia's Tenth Presbyterian Church.

"I listened and was amazed," Jim recalls. "On the spot I decided to make a 'theological investigation.' "

How does a dancing instructor do that? Simple. He goes to the nearest newsstand and buys a book on religion.

Jim laughs about it as he looks back. "Who knows what I could have gotten? Maybe that's why I'm a Calvinist now. God was certainly watching over me."

The news vendor recommended Fulton Oursler's classic, *The Greatest Story Ever Told*.

Jim started reading a little of the book each day. He finished it the next Saturday night (instead of going to another party). Astonished, he laid down the book. From the part of the Barnhouse message he had heard the previous Sunday, Jim knew that eternal life was a free gift.

"The law is not our salvation; it is our condemnation," Barnhouse's words rang in his ears.

Sinking to his knees, Jim Kennedy asked Jesus Christ into his heart. He asked Him to take charge of his life.

"It seemed as if the cross of Christ were erected right there in my bedroom," he says quietly. "I knew I had eternal life and that things were different."

That assurance continued the next day: "Something had happened inside of me. I hadn't seen any visions or heard any voices, but I knew that somehow I was different. God had changed my 'wanter.' Things that I had wanted before I no longer wanted."

No one else was aware of Jim's conversion. He found Christ through one radio program, broadcast from a thousand miles away; and a book whose author was dead.

Some habits instantly dropped out of Jim Kennedy's life. Drinking, swearing, and immorality lost their appeal. Nobody lectured Jim about Christian conduct. In fact, Jim says he did not know any Christians before his conversion—at least none who said they were. Jim notes that if he ever did meet any true Christians before that, "they were secret agents, not ambassadors for Christ."

Jim had gone to work for Arthur Murray after two and one-half years of college. He had always liked dancing. On a whim one day he answered a newspaper ad for a job at the Tampa studio. During the six years he was with Arthur Murray in Tampa he worked his way to the top: instructor; interviewer; analyst; adviser; supervisor; and finally, manager.

He mastered the mambo, samba, tango, rumba, paso doble and other in dances of the fifties. He won trophies and prize money, topping his honors with first place in the Murray national "All-American" contest.

Off hours he chased girls and played Ping-Pong. (He made more points with his "ping-pong diplomacy" with the girls than he did playing table tennis.)

One Friday night a fellow brought a girl friend to the studio for some dancing instruction. An hour before their appointment. Jim wasted no time meeting her.

Later, during a break, he said to the other teachers in the back room: "I just met the young lady that I'm going to marry." He never had said anything like that before.

Anne Lewis was Jim's student for six months. One day she asked him where he went to church.

"You can be just as good a Christian by not going to church as you can by going," he replied.

"No, you can't!" she answered.

"I have never heard that before," Jim protested.

Everyone who worked at the studio agreed with Jim. They thought they were Christians though none of them went to church.

Anne's question lingered in the back of Jim's mind, and it played a part that day when the clock radio roused Jim from his physical—and spiritual—slumber.

Jim did not break down any doors or mount any soapboxes to proclaim the news of his spiritual birth. It was months before he even told Anne about it.

Although she attended church regularly and was "religious," Anne did not know the Lord personally. Jim finished his book and his prayer of commitment and went to a church the very next day.

Soon Jim switched to a Presbyterian congregation. He was warmly welcomed there by a young man who made him promise he would return to the Young People's Bible Study that evening.

Jim was embarrassed to show his ignorance of Scripture, so he spent the afternoon memorizing the names of the books of the Bible. He began memorizing Scripture passages.

Soon Jim memorized the Sermon on the Mount, and he became so sharp in the Young People's Bible Study that the inevitable happened. When the regular teacher left several months later, Jim was put in charge.

His secret finally leaked out to Anne; she was astonished to learn that he was teaching a Bible class.

About a year later God started nudging Jim about the ministry through the elegant lady trimmed in furs on the church doorstep.

The night he phoned the Miami owner to announce he was quitting Arthur Murray, Jim made another decision: He would level with Anne on two counts.

First, he would tell her he had quit his job and was going to study for the ministry. Second, he would ask her to marry him.

If Anne said yes, it would mean she would have to work to help support them (a $13 bank account would not stretch far). It would also mean reversing her firm decision not to marry a minister.

Jim recounted his proposal to Anne in a recent conversation, as if he were still unable to believe her answer:

"She said 'yes'!"

Anne Craig Lewis of Lakeland, Florida, became Mrs. D. James Kennedy on August 25, 1956, in Lakeland's First Presbyterian Church. Jim had just finished his preaching stint at Bethel in Clearwater and would begin classes the next month at Columbia Seminary in Georgia.

As he relived the experience, Jim leaned back in his chair. He spoke with an air of satisfaction.

"It just goes to show, you can't always believe a woman when she says she'll never do something."

3: PASTOR AND PARTNER

Jim Kennedy was born November 3, 1930, in Augusta, Georgia. His father was from the North, his mother from the South. The family lived in Chicago until Jim's high school days.

Jim's father, a glass salesman of Scotch-Irish stock, died in 1971. His mother lives in Tampa. Jim's one brother, George, is an English teacher at a junior college.

Jim's parents were United Methodists. They sent him to Sunday school in Chicago. Jim joined the church and he joined the Boy Scouts. He says scouting was "very meaningful" in his youth. The church was not.

He remembers details of scouting, but he can recall only one incident in his early religious training: the time he was the only pupil in his Sunday school class to show up.

"The teacher said, 'Come on, get in the car,' " Jim muses. "We drove down to a little tiny lake somewhere in Chicago five or ten minutes away. We sat on the grass under a tree by the lake and had our Sunday school lesson. That's the only Sunday school lesson I remember."

As a lad Jim never attended any church camp, nor did he go to an evangelistic service or rally.

Jim was no student, although his grades at Plant

High School in Tampa, where he graduated in 1948, were pretty good.

He enrolled at the University of Tampa. There, for two and a half years, he "majored" in crew, girls, and Ping-Pong.

Soon the Arthur Murray ad caught his eye, and Kennedy dropped out of school for six years.

Jim's college major (he graduated from the University of Tampa in the summer of 1958) was English; he had a music minor. He was the college band drum major and solo clarinetist.

Anne also has musical talent. She taught music at Birmingham Southern College for four years after graduating from the Methodist-related college.

Jim has maintained a lifelong interest in art. He paints and enjoys browsing in art shops (he particularly likes realistic works). He also studies languages "like a hobby"—Greek and Hebrew particularly. He is a history buff.

His musical taste runs to classical compositions. Although there has been some folk music in the Coral Ridge Church on Sunday nights, Jim is not crazy about guitars in the sanctuary.

And what about dancing? Does the old Arthur Murray pro still glide around the floor with his star pupil?

"I refrain for the sake of my testimony," says Jim, "so that no one will be offended."

By the time Jim had given his heart and life to Jesus Christ, he had matured considerably. When he returned to college, he had definite goals. After his conversion his grades soared to straight "A"s.

Jim declares Christ made the difference.

After he received his Bachelor of Divinity degree (cum laude) from Columbia Theological Seminary in

1959, Jim and Anne settled down in Fort Lauderdale. Coral Ridge has been his only pastorate.

Jim's pursuit of academic knowledge has continued.

In 1969 he received the Master of Theology (*summa cum laude*) degree from the Chicago Graduate School of Theology.

The same year he was also awarded an honorary D.D. degree from Trinity College/Evangelical Divinity School, Deerfield, Illinois.

The scholarly clergyman is now nearing completion of requirements for his Ph.D. in religion, to be conferred by New York University. Residency requirements will be met in 1972; he will have spent three summer sessions there in a program stretching over six years.

Why is Jim putting out the time and effort to nail down a Ph.D.?

"There is a need for evangelical ministers to be thoroughly educated and equipped to meet on equal terms anyone with whom they come in contact," Jim believes. "It is increasingly important," he adds, "to dispel the idea there is an inconsistency between evangelism and education."

"There is the notion that the role of evangelist is a sinecure," he points out. Strong scholarship and intellectual acumen *can* go hand in hand with forthright Biblical evangelism.

Christmas to Easter is Florida's "high season," with Fort Lauderdale's already burgeoning population swelling almost double with the influx of part-time residents and fun-seekers from across the nation.

In February, during the midst of this, is the annual minister's clinic. By Easter Monday, Jim sighs, he feels ready for the hospital. Or at least bed rest.

Summer is the slack time in Florida. The heat drives tourists and residents away or into air-conditioned hibernation. Jim has spent nine weeks each summer for the past five years taking courses toward graduate degrees.

When Jim can take his stated day off (Mondays), he enjoys playing tennis with his wife, or perhaps in a foursome. He likes to spend time with his daughter, Jennifer.

A native of Statesville, North Carolina, Jim's wife Anne lived most of her unmarried life in Lakeland, Florida.

She was an active and religious Presbyterian. Her father was an elder. Anne was active in the church youth group. She taught Sunday school and sang in the choir.

After college (she majored in Spanish and minored in music) she took graduate work in elementary education at the University of California at Los Angeles.

She was a success in several careers, but Anne was restless. She was making good money and had many material things, yet something was lacking. Anne tried travel to Europe, then dancing lessons at a certain Tampa studio. . . .

For a while she even began to consider a career as a professional dancer. Anne and Jim sometimes talked about religious beliefs. During the two years they dated they had several disagreements over religion. Both of them attended church.

One day, a while after Jim's conversion experience through the Barnhouse broadcast, he took Anne to a Youth for Christ meeting in St. Petersburg.

Flushed with the glow of a new-found relationship to Christ, Jim was eager to share it. He thought Anne would feel the same way. He asked her to give her testimony. She refused.

"There was a slow, dawning awareness that some-

24

thing was not right," Jim recalls. "Anne did not have a personal knowledge of Christ."

Not long after that, the two went to a small church near Tampa. A young missionary girl spoke of Jesus—her very real Friend. She told of her mission work in India.

The testimony touched Anne's heart. That night, at the end of their date, Jim led Anne in prayer while they sat in the car in front of her home.

Then Anne prayed. There was an inner change as she acknowledged her need of the Savior and made her commitment to Him.

Anne's ministry in the church has been subordinate to Jim's. She sees her role as a teammate. Anne knows a PW (pastor's wife) can easily get uptight over the pace and problems of a busy parish.

Tennis has become her outlet. She plays three times a week. Strictly for fun.

Jim's life as pastor to 2,500 and spiritual advisor to multiplied thousands now heaps heavy demands on him, physically, mentally, and emotionally. It has not always been so to such a degree.

4: A DISCOURAGED YOUNG PASTOR

To go on with our story—people often think successful evangelists are the hotshot, extrovert, super-salesman type. Jim Kennedy isn't.

Nothing could be further from the truth, judging from Jim's natural inclinations.

"Why, I've been on an airplane for three hours and never gotten up enough nerve to say 'good morning' to the person next to me," he confesses.

That's quite an admission from one who has spoken to at least 25,000 ministers and seminarians on how to witness to others about Jesus Christ, who has trained hundreds in his own church to do so, and who has led countless hundreds to the Lord one by one through his own personal witnessing.

What's happening in Fort Lauderdale today is a far cry from the early days when a struggling congregation of forty-five [the beginning of Coral Ridge] met in McNab Elementary School in Fort Lauderdale to hear neophyte Kennedy preach.

Jim actually did not plan to become a full-time parish minister. His initial plan was either to continue graduate study or to go to the mission field in the fall of 1959.

He was not accepted for graduate study at Emory University where he applied, and the mission board turned him down because of his allergies.

At the last minute Jim accepted a call to become the

organizing pastor of the Coral Ridge Presbyterian Church in Fort Lauderdale.

The Coral Ridge charge was hardly an ecclesiastical plum sought after by all the bright young seminary graduates of the class of 1959. Presbyterian pastors in greater Fort Lauderdale felt it was time to start a new church, and the Home Missions Committee of Everglades Presbytery placed some ads in the local papers announcing the beginning of new work in the area. The local pastors took turns preaching to the little flock that responded.

About forty-five people showed up on an average Sunday morning. The services were held at 8:30 A.M. so the ministers could get back to their own churches for services there. Besides, a small Baptist group had the McNab School cafeteria auditorium at the more popular eleven o'clock hour.

Jim does not remember the title of his first sermon in the school-church, but he vividly recalls a remark made by the first woman to greet him after that service.

"I'm a follower of the teachings of Thomas Paine" (the rationalist, good-deeds religionist), she said. Jim did not quite know how to respond to that. His congregation did not quite know how to respond to him, either.

Jim started preaching with all the vim and vigor that usually infuses a fresh, idealistic minister straight out of seminary. His sermons were fervently evangelistic, and he gave altar calls.

To use Jim's words, the people were "turned off in droves." Chalk it up to inexperience and Jim's insensitivity to his audience. His preaching might have gone over big in some areas—but not in sophisticated Fort Lauderdale.

The people were mostly from the North. They were accustomed to subdued preaching and formal services.

After he had been in Fort Lauderdale ten months, the average attendance was down to seventeen souls. The count-down continued.

Interestingly, the little Baptist group that met in the school at eleven o'clock soon folded. So did several other embryo congregations in the immediate area. Some of the seventeen remaining steadies at Coral Ridge were hangers-on from the pre-Kennedy era; others, newcomers, somehow stuck it out.

"I was becoming a little concerned," Kennedy concedes in mock nonchalance.

Actually, he was on the verge of panic. He questioned his call to the ministry.

"I wondered whether the whole thing had been a horrible mistake; it appeared the church was going to go the way the one at 11:00 A.M. did."

And he adds soberly: "Who needs a young minister who takes a new church and drives it right into the ground?"

Jim had an idea in the back of his head that he might gain some new prospects if he did more calling in homes. That was a chore a shy person did not relish, but he thought he ought to do it—and speak about Christ, too, while he was at it.

For good measure Jim took along a deacon when he made his first "evangelistic" house call. To break in easily, he picked a "little old lady" prospect. That should be easy, he thought.

The "little old lady" was not home, but her big, burly, tough-looking son was.

He flung open the door and confronted Kennedy. "Whad-ya-want?" he bellowed, a cigar in the corner of his mouth and a can of beer in his hands.

Jim was paralyzed. He made inane chit-chat about the weather, the news, sports. Then he tried to say something spiritual. "It caught in my throat," Jim now tells timid trainees at his evangelism clinics.

Obviously the call bombed. Kennedy—with one chagrined deacon in tow—sheepishly retreated. In complete disgrace.

Jim realized then that he had no idea how to witness. Moreover, he lacked the courage to try. He vowed he would never, *never* make another call like that. It was just too painful with a layman along to see what a miserable failure he was as a personal evangelist.

He meant it too. Probably few people beyond Fort Lauderdale would know of D. James Kennedy today if he had not received an unexpected phone call one day from a ministerial acquaintance near Decatur, Georgia.

5: A CALL FROM DECATUR

Jim Kennedy had not talked to Kennedy Smartt since Jim's student days at Columbia Seminary. Then, in mid-1960—ten months after Jim and Anne accepted what had turned out to be Jim's only church offer— Ken Smartt telephoned.

Smartt was pastor of a 250-member Presbyterian church one mile from Decatur, Georgia, in the industrial village of Scottdale. Ingleside was the "in" church for the evangelical crowd at Columbia and Jim and Anne had worshiped there often.

Smartt's call could not have come at a better time. Jim was as low as his Coral Ridge congregation was small.

Jim snapped up the chance to come to Decatur for a ten-day series of evangelistic services. He was relieved to get away from his own evangelism blunders at Coral Ridge.

"If the mountain won't come to Mohammed, then Mohammed would go to the mountain," Jim reasoned. He figured he might have better luck preaching for decisions in another town.

Jim had preached in Smartt's church once before, when he was attending Columbia. Jim had been impressed by the Ingleside Church, and by Ken's easy style and direct proclamation of the Gospel.

Ken Smartt had been impressed with Kennedy too.

He recalled how Jim had shared his unusual testimony about the Barnhouse broadcast. Ken knew Jim had been soundly converted and had led Anne to the Lord.

He was also aware that Jim had an unusual ministry to Willie, a Columbia student from Sweden.

One day Jim and Willie were walking between the red brick buildings on the serene, oak- and hard-wood-shaded campus. Willie seemed to understand nothing about the real meaning of salvation. Jim shared his testimony.

Some classmates were incensed. This was a "great discourtesy" to Willie, they claimed, an affront to his intelligence and sensibility. The campus buzzed with news of Jim's continuing witness to the young Swede.

Willie made a decision for Jesus Christ and joined Ingleside Church. It was natural then that when Ken wanted to invite an evangelistic minister to Decatur he should think about his friend, Jim Kennedy.

"Here's a guy who's knowledgeable about personal work—he led a seminary student to Christ—and he has some insights to give me," reckoned Smartt, who is six years older than Jim and also a Columbia Seminary graduate.

The elder Kennedy placed the life-changing call to the younger Kennedy and invited him to conduct the preaching mission at Ingleside. Jim Kennedy accepted. (Jim tells friends they can distinguish between

31

the two Kennedys—the other Kennedy was "Smartt.")

Jim pulled up to Ken's colonial-style, square-framed church with its traditional steeple and white columns on a nippy April day.

He greeted his friend, Ken.

"Hi," responded the husky, fair-complected native of Lookout Mountain, Tennessee, to his visitor from Fort Lauderdale. "You're going to preach every evening and call every day—face to face, eyeball to eyeball." Smartt's blue eyes twinkled. "I've saved all the tough nuts for you [to crack] ... "

"Oh, Oh! I've been trapped!" sputtered Jim inwardly. His heart sank like a sack of sand thrown off a wharf.

The idea that he would be expected to do house-to-house visitation had not occurred to Jim Kennedy.

He was thinking of his late—and anything but great—witnessing cop-out in Fort Lauderdale when he and his deacon turned tail and fled.

Ken and Jim set off together on the first of dozens of calls they made as a team of two during that preaching mission. Ken does not remember details of that first visit. Jim Kennedy does. It left an indelible impression on Jim.

"In ten minutes I had succeeded in infuriating the person we called on," Jim shudders. "Then Ken took over the conversation and led him to Christ in fifteen minutes."

During the next ten days fifty-three other persons made professions of faith during the evening preaching services. Almost all of them had first made decisions with Ken Smartt during the visits in their homes.

Jim credits the conversions to Ken Smartt's able and smooth personal witnessing during the calls.

"My life was changed by sitting there watching Ken do that," Jim says. "It was a very astonishing experience. I was more than impressed; I was awestruck. It was almost as if that man had some magical powers. I asked him how he had learned to do that. It was amazing.

"He said, 'A year ago I didn't know how to do it at all.'

"I couldn't believe it. 'How did you learn?' I asked.

" 'Well, the evangelist that we had last year really *was* an evangelist,' Ken Smartt explained. 'His name was Bill Iverson. Iverson was made of stern stuff. A Davidson athletic star, he was known for his hard charging—both on the football field and in personal witnessing.

" 'There was no neutral ground with Bill. One day a man told him he was an atheist. Bill shot back at him a question—about how long he had been running around with some woman.

" 'Bill knew the man was afraid to believe in God because of his moral misbehavior.

" 'The man in question was flabbergasted. He burst into tears wondering how Bill Iverson knew. Bill talked to the man. He repented and received Christ.

" 'Of course, not everyone reacted that positively to Iverson. People either melted, or they hated him. I

33

learned a lot of my boldness from Bill Iverson.' "

Ken Smartt's story about the events that took place during the preaching mission is a little different than Jim Kennedy's. He doesn't recall it from the same perspective. He says Jim didn't just sit back and watch the whole time. At the end of the week, each of them took out an elder in separate teams and made calls. Jim was doing the witnessing, Ken says.

Today the Kennedy whose last name is "Smartt" uses the Coral Ridge Evangelism Explosion program in his church. And when he and the other Kennedy are out together and the other Kennedy begins to witness, Kennedy Smartt no longer sees a need to take the lead away from him. His pupil has learned well.

6: CORAL RIDGE PIONEERS

Jim went back to Coral Ridge with new confidence and a buoyant spirit.

"I had seen it done," Kennedy says, referring to the visible results of personal evangelism coupled with strong Biblical preaching that he had seen work in the Decatur preaching mission.

"I started doing exactly what I had seen . . . I even began to sound like Ken Smartt."

Jim started making calls in Fort Lauderdale—again, but he went out alone. The idea of taking someone along—as a trainee—for the moment had dropped entirely out of his thinking. Perhaps it was repressed, he suggests, in light of the traumatic experience with the cigar-chewing, beer-swilling "little old lady" who had met him and his deacon at the door.

Jim followed the Smartt pattern—presenting the Gospel in the home—for at least a year. People responded. He led several persons to Christ every week. Many joined the church. Declining attendance bottomed out and the congregation began to grow.

"People responded in Fort Lauderdale just like they did in Decatur—to my utter amazement," Kennedy recalls.

Eventually Jim saw that he could only witness to a small percentage of the people in the area. He was only one man, and he could only make so many calls in a given amount of time. He knew he would have to train others to witness if ever Fort Lauderdale was to be reached for Christ.

The first man to go out with Jim was an elderly gentleman who had been a Christian most of his life. Victor Wierman was his name. Now in his mid 70s, Vic had always wanted to know how to witness.

Vic—who still makes some calls on his own—went out with Jim for four or five months. He observed Jim in action during fifteen to twenty calls.

"I thought he never was going to get out of the nest and try his wings," Jim smiles, "but he finally did."

When Vic made his first presentation of the Gospel, he soloed. Kennedy did not go. Vic had learned well. His witnessing was an immediate success.

Vic is but one of many Coral Ridge members who have a long lineage of spiritual descendants. Jim thinks Vic's "family" easily numbers in the hundreds.

A number of the persons Vic led to Christ have themselves been "fantastically successful"—as Jim puts it—in reaching others. That's how an individual's influence multiplies and grows.

For example, the Byron Smiths first visited Coral Ridge Church because they were looking for a good Sunday school for their children. About a year later Vic Wierman invited Byron to a dinner of the church men—then followed the invitation up by making an appointment to call in the Smith home.

Byron vividly remembers that evening. He accepted Christ. "It was a dramatic thing," he says, "to know the assurance of Heaven. It was the first time I could make an intelligent decision."

Vic had used the standard questions: *"Have you come to a place in your spiritual life where you know for certain that if you were to die today you would go to Heaven?"*; and *"Suppose you were to die today and stand before God and He were to say to you, 'Why should I let you into My Heaven?' what would you say?"*

Byron had no assurance and gave a typical "works" answer. He based his hope of salvation on hoped-for favor with God through good deeds and moral living rather than on the unmerited grace of God and the righteousness of Christ.

Vic carefully explained the plan of salvation to Byron as they sat in the Smiths' living room in the front part of the house. It had a glass wall. Never mind; when Vic suggested they pray, Byron was not in the least bit self-conscious. The two men knelt in front of the floor-to-ceiling window.

"I wasn't aware that I was in a fish bowl or on stage," Smith recalls with mild amusement.

Six months later Smith was in training (the Evangelism Explosion program was operating then). He remained active in the program until he and his family moved to Cumberland, Maryland, in 1969.

In Fort Lauderdale the Smiths left spiritual children, grandchildren, and great-grandchildren galore. Example: "Grandson" Larry King, 19, a student at Covenant College, is planning full-time Christian service. He was reached for Christ by a man reached by Byron.

That is not all. Byron, an interior design and color consultant, lost no time getting busy with personal work in Cumberland where the Smiths now attend church. There is a training program going there; twenty-five people were already equipped to present Christ by mid-1971. After only one year of Evangelism Explosion training, the church membership is growing nicely. Some family usually professes faith in Christ every week.

Vic Wierman, meantime, feels tremendously blessed to know that he played a part in the divine chain of redemption that has linked so many to the Savior.

Jim Kennedy also praises the second Coral Ridge pioneer who learned to witness by making calls with him. "Dr. Freeman Springer has been tremendously fruitful," Kennedy says. The spiritual children, grandchildren, and step-children (those won by people he has trained) of Freeman and Dottie Springer would almost certainly count into the thousands—if any accurate record could be kept.

Freeman was reared in a "Christian" home, he says, and went through the usual procession of Sunday school, catechism class, and confirmation. His religion was perfunctory and zestless.

As an adult he visited many churches but never settled down and dug in. During the late 1950s he became concerned about what he believed was a drift toward liberalism in this country—both in its government and in the churches.

One night he and his wife, Dottie, attended an anti-Communism rally. Jim Kennedy happened to give the invocation.

"I heard more in two minutes during that prayer than I usually heard in an entire Sunday morning service," Freeman relates.

Not surprisingly, Freeman and Dottie visited Coral Ridge. They found it friendly. Jim "seemed to believe what he was preaching," they say.

After four Sundays they decided to join. Freeman felt he needed to iron out some things that were on his mind—matters like dancing and social drinking that he considered important to his practice and to their social life. The Springers invited Jim over to provide answers in light of what the church taught.

Freeman did not get very far with his questions. Jim zapped him with two of his own. About eternal life and how you can have it.

Freeman said he had tried to obey the Ten Commandments and follow the Golden Rule, but he was jolted when Jim told him a person gets to Heaven by almost the opposite way.

Ten minutes later Jim had explained that works without saving faith accomplish nothing and that eternal life is the free gift of God through His Son.

Freeman dedicated his life to Christ and Dottie rededicated hers. Without a moment's hesitation Freeman can tell you the date: April 3, 1962.

"The Bible became truth overnight," he testifies.

The Springers joined Coral Ridge Church right away; it was then a congregation of 113.

Before long Jim told Freeman he should share his faith. He asked him to go out calling with him on Thursday nights.

Jim took Freeman out four times. No training program or materials had yet been developed. The fifth time Freeman went out he took Dottie. The two of them called on one of Freeman's patients. Both the man and his wife accepted Christ.

The experience was so spiritually invigorating that the Springers—sometimes together, sometimes with other partners—have been making evangelistic calls almost every Thursday since.

Dentist Springer has conducted clinics for ministers and laymen throughout the country. Each year he trains four persons in Evangelism Explosion techniques. Most are maturing in their faith and are winning others.

Springer, 51, a talkative man who likes sports, hunting, and fishing, has won to Christ at least three persons who have set their sights on the ministry. One already has a church; the second is in seminary; the third is a lay preacher.

People make professions of faith very frequently, Freeman told an inquirer.

Springer, a graduate of Marquette University Dental School, has also found that complete trust in Christ brings serendipities to his personal life.

He began tithing immediately after he and Dottie joined the church. The day after he sent in the first check, he notes, money due from patients for several years began coming in. After the first year of tithing, he had a 10 per cent increase in his business.

His clientele has kept increasing every year though Dr. Springer spends more time away from the practice.

Does Freeman witness on the job? Like when he has a patient's mouth pried open so he can't talk back?

That depends. Freeman tries to be sensitive to the spiritual condition of those he sees. He speaks to patients as he feels led by the Spirit. If there is a spark of interest, he may make an appointment to see the patient privately at lunch or on a Thursday night.

Freeman stresses the centrality of the Bible in living the Christian life:

"God's Word gives the power to witness and live the life; also to win others . . . God delights in showing us His power in many little ways."

Freeman has participated in all six of the annual ministers' training clinics held at Coral Ridge each February. He has led or taken part in mini-clinics for ministers and laymen in Dallas (Presbyterian), Denver (Baptist), Chicago (Reformed Church in America), and Des Moines (Lutheran).

Jim Kennedy is not exaggerating when he says Freeman Springer is "tremendously fruitful" as a disciple of Jesus Christ. During the first two years that Freeman made evangelistic calls, 225 persons made commitments. ("But put the emphasis on the Lord, not me," Freeman cautions. "I'm only His instrument.")

Freeman lost count of his spiritual children in 1964. "I didn't want to play the numbers game," he explains.

The third man to learn the emerging evangelism method under the tutelage of Kennedy is now pastor of Coral Springs Presbyterian Church, a daughter congregation of Coral Ridge.

The Reverend Ross Bair is his name. He was the first man from Coral Ridge to enter the Gospel ministry. Before he started the mission church, Ross served on the staff at Coral Ridge.

Ross Bair has led hundreds to Christ.

Kennedy took Jacob Magenheimer, now 72, under his wing for witness training in 1965, the year after he had signed a visitor's card at Coral Ridge. He was Jim's fourth personal trainee.

A retired vice-president of the Chase Manhattan Bank, Magenheimer was convinced by a Fort Lauderdale golfing buddy that they ought to "join a church, get involved, and do something."

A member of the Coral Ridge witnessing team called on Magenheimer's friend first. The caller met resistance over questions about the Virgin Birth, who the woman was that Cain married, etc.

Finally the caller spouted in exasperation: "Why is it so difficult for you to believe?"

He answered: "If you think you're having a hard

time with me, just wait until you call on Magenheimer!"

Two days later—by special request—Kennedy called on Magenheimer.

Jake describes the encounter in a little booklet he uses as a tract: "My Answers Were Wrong."

After the usual niceties, Jim zeroed in with the two questions. Jake decided to trick him with the "right" answers:

"Well, pastor, I believe in the Ten Commandments, also the Golden Rule. I have been honorably employed; I have two fine children, and they are still married to the same people they married originally. I have five grandchildren, all of whom love their grandpa very much. . . .

"I may, of course, have some sins against me, but I have had no trouble with the police. I have a good moral background, and I believe in God. I may have to wait in line a little bit, but I honestly feel God will let me in."

Jim shook his head. "You have said 'I' ten times."

He went on, using Ephesians 2: 8, 9 (for by grace you are saved); Romans 3: 23 (all have sinned); and John 3: 16 (God so loved the world) to show Jake that he had been trusting in himself—not Christ—to get into Heaven.

Continuing with Romans 10: 9, 10 (by the heart man believes and with the mouth confesses salvation), Jim led Jake to turn over his life to Christ.

"From that day on I have had so many blessings I just can't count them," Jake says enthusiastically.

Soon Jim asked Jake to go calling with him. After about five calls and some mock witnessing-training sessions, Jake was told to find a younger man to accompany him and have a go at making a call himself.

Jake first presented the Gospel to a couple who were on the verge of divorce. The woman had signed a pew card indicating she needed help.

Jake tried the direct approach: "You're in trouble," he said to the husband when he admitted to Jake that he had been gone from home about ten weeks and had just returned.

The man, acknowledging his marriage was all but wrecked, fell on his knees. He pounded the floor with his fists and pleaded for help.

Jake led both the man and his wife to Christ that night. They became active in the church.

"Nobody knows what a terrific feeling it is to know that God has made you His messenger," Jake affirms gratefully, looking back on years of spiritual service. "You have to experience it to fully understand."

He says he has witnessed to somebody, somewhere, every day since that first conversion experience.

In 1966 Jake moved to Coral Gables to be nearer his grown children and their families. He started attending Granada Presbyterian Church there.

A young evangelical minister named Robert Ostenson had just become pastor. Few, if any, in the church knew how to witness effectively.

Jake showed them how, much to Ostenson's pleasure. By 1971 the church, using the Evangelism Explosion program, was adding a dozen or more new members each month.

Jake has also put the Coral Ridge method to work in Dade County jail, where he has witnessed almost every Sunday for the last three years. About fifty inmates profess Christ each week, according to Jake.

A spiritual activist, Jake also visits the Armed Forces Induction Center each Wednesday and frequently speaks in rescue missions, rehabilitation camps for alcoholics, and at Christian Business Men's committee meetings.

Kennedy's wife, Anne, is truly another pioneer of the Coral Ridge Evangelism Explosion, though she might not think of herself in quite those terms. She became trained in personal witnessing almost by accident. Jim often had her accompany him on calls because it gave them a chance to be together during evenings when Anne would otherwise have been home alone.

She has staunchly refused to accept leadership roles in women's work or as an officer in the church. Her advice to wives: "Don't overshadow your husband."

She definitely believes a pastor's wife should be a co-worker. The two should work as a team, she feels.

Before Jennifer, their only child, was born in 1962, Anne went with Jim on most of his calls. She took no active role, other than being friendly. Yet all the while she was learning—almost unconsciously—from Jim.

After a while she began making some calls on her own. She led persons to the Savior. She preferred to go alone (she still does), and admits she is a little scared even now while she waits on the doorstep after punching the doorbell.

In addition to training many laymen, for five years she has taken pastors with her as trainees during the annual ministers' clinics in Fort Lauderdaie. Jim praises her as a thoroughly skilled evangelist.

Why does she do it? "It's exciting," she says, her blue-green eyes dancing.

"To see somebody make a profession of faith is nice, but the greatest thing is seeing that person grow within a week—to know it's for eternity."

Many of the people tapped for Christian service during the pioneer years of the Evangelism Explosion were middle-aged men and women. Wierman and Magenheimer were in their mid-sixties. Springer was in his early forties.

One man began training for the ministry at age 52. Doyle Hulse decided he wanted to go into full-time Christian service the first night Jim took him out on a visit.

"He was a very carnal man," Jim recalls. "I was amazed when he even said he wanted to go out on a visit. He seemed to have very, very little spiritual perception or concern."

When Jim got home he told Anne: "I almost fell out of the car when I was on the way home tonight. You know what Doyle Hulse said? He said he'd like to be a missionary!"

Sure enough, Doyle Hulse wound up in the ministry. A mechanic, he needed to complete a year of college and then three years of seminary before he was ordained. Now he teaches Bible at a small college in Mississippi and pastors a church. He is now a saintly man, being used by God.

Stories of God's redeeming love and empowering for service abound. The threads are interwoven through countless lives and across several continents.

Training techniques have gradually become more sophisticated. Team training and practice sessions are innovations that have seemed to work. Just as the young man who accompanied Magenheimer learned to present the Gospel during a call and then found a new teammate and trained him, each trainee learns to witness and then teaches another how to do it.

Two points stand out clearly from interviews with early pioneers of the Coral Ridge Evangelism Explosion.

One: The laymen have been extremely blessed by being used of God to win others for Christ. *Two*: Almost to a man or woman, the callers have continued to witness regularly through the years; some now span almost a decade of spiritual service.

One of the most striking features of the Kennedy Evangelism Explosion is the compelling way those who are won become ambassadors and missionaries for Jesus Christ wherever they go.

7: TRAINING OTHERS

Even before Jim started taking men along with him on evangelistic calls, he was aware of the need to train others in personal witnessing. His original plan was to teach lay evangelists through classes that he conducted at the church.

Though the classes got off the ground, the people did not. Nobody learned how to witness.

He got together a dozen interested people. They studied for six weeks. Jim sent them out. So he thought.

They all went home.

They were afraid to face the unknown. "Fear," says Jim, "is the main roadblock keeping would-be-witnesses from communicating their faith." Those in that first class lacked confidence and practical know-how; they had only a book knowledge.

Undaunted, Jim whipped together another class. This time they were indoctrinated for twelve weeks. A few went out. They tried to witness, but they soon met situations that they were not equipped by their training to handle.

They gave up.

Jim tried again with a still longer class of twenty weekly meetings. To his knowledge, not *one* person was converted as a result. One very brilliant woman did learn how to witness through the classes, Jim recalls, but she did not win any converts.

Finally it hit him: The people had to be *shown* how to witness—not just told how.

Jim is fond of explaining his revelation.

"Suppose," he begins, "that someone who wants to become a pilot takes classroom instruction:

"After fifty hours of classes does he lack know-how? He would know a tremendous amount about flying an airplane. Book know-how! Yet there is a certain kind of know-how he lacks. He has not had the actual experience and feel of the flying plane, the feel of the elements reacting against it."

The feel and experience for evangelism gained in on-the-job training, like the feel and experience of flying gained in the cockpit, build confidence and know-how. Coral Ridge evangelists are successful because they have been *shown* how to witness.

When a person recruits flying students he does it person-to-person, so only people interested and capable of learning to fly sign up for lessons. Person-to-person recruitment of trainees for lay evangelism helps screen out those people who would not be suited to witnessing. Personal recruitment helps insure a successful program that contains interested, personable trainees.

Kennedy learned (the hard way) that it is not a good idea to just invite people to come to the calling classes. He did that at first. Few came. People need to be recruited individually.

"We sometimes get up in the pulpit and exhort the people," he tells other clergymen. "It's just like saying to people, 'You ought to fly an airplane. You should have been flying an airplane long before now. Therefore, get out and start flying today!'

"Not everyone can learn to fly, nor should they. Not everyone in a given group can witness either. A trainee has to want to do it to be successful.

"You don't just give exhortation and mere class instruction either. You take the people with you. They learn to take the controls gradually. You do it piece-meal."

Jim was so taken with his idea of on-the-job training that at first he stopped the personal evangelism classes. Thus began the era of training, on a personal basis, men like Wierman, Springer, Bair, and Magenheimer.

After training five or six evangelists, Jim realized he could not possibly train everyone himself.

What's more, he saw that he did not need to do so.

"Wilbur and Orville didn't teach everybody how to fly," Jim reasons impeccably.

"It's more important to train a soulwinner than to win a soul," Jim asserts as part of his philosophy. "I think that concept alone could revolutionize a lot of ministries."

"Once he arrived at the principle that people should become *disciplers* as well as disciples, Jim reinstituted the classes. This time he invited people personally rather than announcing the class from the pulpit. He asked each one he had already trained to bring two trainees.

The pendulum had swung from one end to the other—and back to center: from classes only, to no classes, to classes and on-the-job training combined.

This latter combination is what makes Kennedy's Evangelism Explosion attractive to lay evangelists. Practical knowledge and experience conquer fear.

Jim explained to Carey Moore of *Decision* magazine how the program works (June, 1970, issue, page 9): "I began a program which has continued for the past

49

[nine] years, taking out one individual until he has confidence to witness to others, and then another, and another. After the people are trained, they in turn can train others."

The new classes suffered from a lack of prepared material. Then someone asked, "Why not write this down so we can study it during the week?"

Jim decided that was a good idea. Trouble was, Jim didn't really remember what he said when he was out on calls. He had to begin to listen to himself.

"It must have taken me a month or more to try to listen to what I was saying to these people—the subjects and the order—and to try to keep mental notes," Jim said later.

Jim realized there was a definite pattern to his witnessing presentation. He kept notes on what he said during each call—how people answered, and what they thought. He put his notes into manuscript form, and this became the core material for the Evangelism Explosion program as it is presently taught at Coral Ridge twice a year.

Each training program now lasts four and a half months. One program begins in the fall, the other in the early spring. Sandwiched between the two sessions, in February, is a training clinic for ministers.

At Coral Ridge Presbyterian Church, the lay evangelism classes are only about half an hour long. Classes are held on the same day people go out on visitation. That way trainees don't get any ivory-tower classroom instruction; they go out—as observers—on the very first day, along with the very first class. Evangelists-in-training observe until they are ready to take over and do various parts of the total presentation.

Study assignments are given at each class for the

following week when trainees (and their trainers) assemble after calling for a lecture on the topic of the day.

The size of the classes is strictly limited to the available trainers. Jim encourages those previously trained to keep right on coming to subsequent classes —with two trainees under their wing.

A person becomes a trainee, spends four and a half months or more learning the presentation of the Gospel in clear and understandable terms, gains experience at actual presentation, and then finds two people he can take with him to train for four and a half months. This spiritual multiplication is what makes this method of evangelism an "explosion."

That way, Jim says, the total pool of active, trained callers does not dry up. More than 500 in the Coral Ridge congregation had been trained by the summer of 1971.

As Jim consciously began listening to himself ask the questions and present the Gospel, a skeletal outline emerged. First in his mind, then on paper.

This outline was the beginning of what now is a complete training program that includes a book, *Evangelism Explosion,* a package of cassette tapes, *Kennedy Cassettes on Lay Evangelism,* and several films. (See pages 127 and 128 for information on where to obtain products about the Kennedy program.)

None of the Coral-Ridge-trained evangelists says exactly the same thing every time, but they do follow a basic outline. So does everyone who witnesses consistently, Jim claims.

Other Gospel presentations will work, also, but Jim cautions that they should be Biblically sound and thorough—"the full-orbed Gospel." They should be

51

adapted to fit the people the caller is trying to reach.

Jim is sold on the two questions [*"Have you come to a place in your spiritual life where you know for certain that if you were to die today you would go to Heaven?"* and *"Suppose you were to die today and stand before God and He were to ask you, 'Why should I let you into My Heaven?' what would you say?"*] used in the Coral Ridge plan. Their purpose, he explains, is to get the listener to admit that he does not have eternal life and that he has not understood and accepted the Gospel (if that is the case).

The wording is important; they do not rule the person in or out of the Kingdom. They are reasonably fail-safe. If a question is worded in such a way that the right answer can be faked, then the caller is left with nothing more to say. His prospect may, in fact, not really believe what he has just said, parrot fashion, in reply.

The first question, *"Have you come to a place in your spiritual life where you can say you know for certain that if you were to die today you would go to Heaven?"* is not threatening. And it may sort out, early in the call, the Christian from the non-Christian. The Christian will answer with an affirmative reply and possibly with a comment on how he knows.

Jim surmises from a decade of experience that some 90 per cent of non-believers do not even know that they *can* have assurance of eternal salvation.

The second question rather quickly separates those who are trusting in works or themselves for salvation from those who trust Christ alone: *"Suppose you were to die tonight and stand before God, and He were to ask you, 'Why should I let you into My Heaven?' what would you say?"*

Once the caller finds out where the person is

spiritually, he presents the Gospel guided by the outline and material that he now knows and understands because it's a part of him through training and practice. Unless, of course, the responses indicate the person already is a Christian. In that case, the call proceeds on the lines of sharing and encouragement. The caller knows how to do that too!

The evangelistic call closes, when it is appropriate, by bringing the person to a commitment to Christ, and with cordial expressions of interest and friendship.

On training nights, when the teams have completed their outings, they return to the church for a report session.

"These are really exciting," Kennedy notes.

Some trainees catch on to the presentation with the ease of a duck gliding into water. A few bump and jerk like a square-wheeled cart.

Those who have mastered the techniques swear that anyone—no matter how shy or how minuscule his Bible knowledge—can become a skilled evangelist.

Byron Smith and Doug Ludeman are cases in point.

Six months after Byron Smith made a commitment to Christ on January 28, 1967, while kneeling in his glass-walled living room [see chapter five], he was in training.

"I had no spiritual background," he told a friend four years later. "I knew no Scripture. My prayer life had consisted of 'Now I lay me. . . .' "

Byron completed the four-and-a-half-month training program, without even seeing the Gospel presented during a call. Though he had gone out with his trainer numerous times, none of the calls had resulted in an actual presentation.

The annual ministers' clinic was set to begin soon

after Byron's training session ended. Jim needed all the trainers he could muster to teach the hundred or so clergymen about to descend on Fort Lauderdale. He asked Byron to be an instructor.

Byron demurred. He had not yet made a full presentation or nailed down a decision, he protested.

"We're counting on you; you've got to," Jim said firmly.

So Byron made a date to try another call. He asked Paul Settle, then a staff minister at Coral Ridge, to go with him. Settle presented the Gospel.

Byron still was not ready. The day the pastors' clinic opened, he decided to practice on a friend. Alone.

The friend was a patient in a psychiatric hospital. Byron says he accepted Christ and that there was "a marked change in him at that time."

Byron Smith, who has since moved to Maryland, continues to be an effective and fruitful worker for the Lord. He recently conducted a mini-clinic for a Christian Missionary and Alliance Church in Morgantown, West Virginia.

Douglas Ludeman is another successful—but late-blooming—Coral-Ridge-trained evangelist. He came to know Christ after talking with Jim Kennedy in his church study in 1962. Soon Doug and his wife, Joanne —who had accepted Christ a month or two before— moved to Fort Lauderdale from Miami. They joined Coral Ridge in January of 1963. The church then had about 250 members.

As a new and growing Christian, Doug wanted to serve Christ. He asked Jim what he could do. Kennedy gave him an Evangelism Explosion worksheet and challenged him to turn out for the Coral Ridge training program.

Doug assented. He made his first call with a young

man named Ben Morgan, who had been a member of Coral Ridge for several years.

As Doug remembers it, Morgan rather muddled the presentation of the Gospel, but the man they called on accepted Christ as his Savior anyway.

Doug was impressed: "I was overwhelmed the Lord used this man [Morgan] to lead another to Himself."

Toward the end of his class series, Doug Ludeman tried presenting the Gospel. He describes his feelings in one word: "petrified."

The call went badly.

In fact, the episode was so upsetting Doug completely dropped out of the evangelism program for four or five months.

Determined to learn, Doug then decided to go through the whole four and a half months of training all over again.

Patient persistence paid off. Doug Ludeman began evangelism training in April of 1963. He won his first convert in October, 1964.

Doug concedes he is very shy. Surprisingly, perhaps, though he is not the salesman type, he has a sales-type job (he is now vice-president of a Richmond, Virginia, bank).

Kennedy confirms Ludeman's taciturnity. He mentions how Doug, after finally mastering the Gospel presentation, found the warm-up, get-acquainted preliminaries of a call more difficult than presenting the Gospel.

Even now Doug admits he "still doesn't feel comfortable" making calls. Not every person does.

Yet one of the persons God touched through Doug Ludeman was to become the leader of an exciting outreach program at Coral Ridge Church—perhaps its most vital tie to the thousands of restless young adults in the community.

Of that experience Doug says: "I feel rather like the shoe salesman who led Dwight L. Moody to the Lord. . . . But the Lord did use me."

Who make better evangelists, pastors or lay people? Men or women?

Jim Kennedy will pick his veteran lay witnesses over the professionals any day. He contends persons who have been in the Evangelism Explosion program seven to nine years "are far more expert than most ministers."

He adds: "I have some laymen—and especially laywomen—in this program I wouldn't trade for one hundred ministers chosen at random."

Why? Clergymen sometimes have hangups and inhibitions that slow them down. Also, what clergyman has had nine years of weekly training in personal evangelism?

Anne Kennedy—herself a ten-year veteran of Coral Ridge evangelism—documented this one night during a call.

She was the trainer for a certain minister—who will remain nameless—attending a recent clergy clinic at Coral Ridge. It was the last night—his turn to present the Gospel.

After about two hours of meandering all over the theological map, the cleric sought to clinch the decision.

Minister: "Do you think you have eternal life now?"

Man (in wheel chair): "No, I don't have eternal life. I told you in the beginning I don't have eternal life. I didn't have it then, and I don't have it now. You haven't told me how I can get it!"

Anne, who was supposed to be quiet and let the

minister do the talking, was taut with anxiety. She could not stand it a moment longer.

Taking over the fumbled ball, she started at the beginning with the Gospel presentation—and led the man to Christ.

Jim has high praise for all his women callers. He says they tend to be more capable than the men. Women, incidentally, make up about 60 per cent of the Coral Ridge lay evangelists. The ladies, he says, are likely to study the materials more than the men do. In general they are more sensitive to the feelings and needs of others.

Jim summed up his feeling during a moment of reflection: "What's so exciting about this is that during our evangelism clinics, without any exception our laymen have always brought more people to Christ than the ministers, secretaries of evangelism, professional evangelists, evangelism professors at seminaries, and heads of denominations who have attended these clinics.

"Our lay people have not only had classes in evangelism for years; they have had years of experience.

"These people really act as seed pods when they go out; it's amazing what they do."

8: FIRE FROM THE CORAL RIDGE PULPIT

Jim was relaxed and in an expansive mood. He was speaking more fluently than when he had been talking about himself and his past.

Now he was telling about the Coral Ridge Evangelism Explosion. He hopped from point to point, strategy to execution, insight to evaluation with the ease of a taxi driver threading his way through the labyrinthine back streets of a huge city.

The subject turned to his preaching schedule and his favorite Scripture passages.

If he had but one sermon to give, what would it be? Jim thought for a long moment. Then came the confident reply: "How You Can Live Forever." Text: I John 5: 13.

His favorite chapter in the Bible is Romans 3, especially verses 19-31. "This chapter contains the most succinct distillation of the Gospel in the entire Scriptures. If I could only preach from one chapter, it would be Romans 3."

Kennedy is a strong preacher; his messages are studded with lively illustrations and quotations from historians, the Church Fathers, poets, and men of letters. Each sermon is interlaced with Scripture references. Indeed, the Bible forms the framework of every sermon.

Jim roughly follows the Christian year; he preaches

"educational evangelism" topically on Sunday mornings. His Sunday evening messages are exegetical, with strong doctrinal content. He notes that parishioners receive spiritual food throughout the week "so I don't have to do the whole thing Sunday mornings."

Jim's droll sense of humor frequently pops up in the pulpit. His sermonic prowess belies the spoof he tells about the lady who gushed at the door: "Oh, Dr. Kennedy, every one of your sermons is better than the next!"

Assurance of salvation and the truth of God's Word are central themes in Jim's preaching.

"What we need today is the proclamation of the truth of God's Word," he said in his January 7, 1968, sermon, "The Future of the Church." "The Gospel is *still* the power of God unto salvation and it is *still* the most glorious Good News that this world has ever heard.

"I had the privilege, in the last two weeks, of talking to a man over seventy-five years old who has been in church all his life, and he had never even so much as grasped the faintest inkling of what the Gospel was! Jesus, he thought, was but a man and a sinner; salvation was by presenting one's good works to God and maybe one might get to Heaven, perhaps!

"But it was with tears of rejoicing moistening his cheeks that he embraced Christ as his Savior and received the gift of eternal life. Yesterday again, with clouded eyes, he told me that he knew that he had eternal life. Would to God that somebody would have told him that sixty years ago! A soul saved but a lifetime lost to the Kingdom of God."

On evangelism: "I hope there will be fashioned here an army, committed and dedicated soldiers of Christ, who can sing 'Onward, Christian Soldiers' without being utter hypocrites, and who will go out into this city and reap such a multitude of people and bring them to the cross of Christ that this whole town will be aghast at what has happened to it.

"Someone has said, 'We don't talk about religion or politics' . . . Who is it that has had the audacity to make such a statement? . . . Surely that is a lie that was fashioned in the very forges of hell."

On missions: "The new site that we have is without any question the choicest church site in all of this state—and perhaps in all of this nation—for it is in a tremendously growing area: the 'gold coast' of Florida.

"Do you know that there is enough money in the gold coast of Fort Lauderdale to support the world mission enterprise of the Church itself, many times better than it is used to being supported? By the grace of God I hope to get a piece of the gold coast in Africa and the Orient!

"Some years ago we had a missionary doctor, who was a surgeon in Korea, speak from this pulpit. . . . He said they were trying desperately to get a new hospital in that leprosarium but it would cost $500,000. I vowed that night that by the grace of God there would come a day that, for such a cause as this, we could say to such a man as that, 'After the service, stop in the office and pick up your hospital.' "

Jim has worked hard to educate his people about good stewardship habits. He has set the pace by endeavoring to increase the percentage of his own giving to the Lord's work each year.

He finds it impossible to outgive God! "It's hard to keep giving more because God keeps giving so much that the percentage keeps dropping down."

Some Coral Ridge members give up to 50 per cent of their income to the church; one woman (who lives on her husband's income) gives 100 per cent of her earnings as a maid to the church. Jim states that 61 per cent of the church's pledging units give a tithe or more. (At one time, when the church was smaller, up to 80 per cent of the members tithed, Jim avers.)

In his 1968 (November 10) annual stewardship sermon, Jim started off on a light note: "A wife asked her husband, 'Can you give me a little money?' He responded, 'Yes, how little?' That sort of typifies the attitude of many church people when it comes around to stewardship time.

"There was an evangelist once who had wires connected to all of the seats. Everybody that was to give $100 was to stand. When he asked the question, 'How many people are willing to give $100?' he pushed a button and electricity flowed into the seats. There was a great response but later the sexton found three Scotsmen electrocuted!"

Several minutes later Jim was dead serious: "It has often been said that Christ spoke more about money and possessions than He did about Heaven— or any other subject, for that matter. Was Jesus unspiritual? Or did He, in fact, so understand the spiritual realm and the nature of man that He knew that all sorts of supposed piety, which does not get down to where a man lives and what he owns, is only hypocrisy?

"I am absolutely convinced that any person who has not come to the place of getting honest with God about his money has not gotten honest with God about anything else. . . ."

Jim calls prayer "one of the real struggles of the Christian life." He has never found it easy—although he prays at stated times daily. He says prayer is absolutely vital for a strong Christian life.

Thus the sermon, "Prayer, the Noblest Art," was forged on the anvil of Jim's experience: "Prayer is not only a universal instinct, it is also an art. As theology is the queen of the sciences, prayer is the noblest of the arts. Surpassing music, painting, sculpture, is the divine art of prayer. It is that personal linkage with the eternal, the communion with power unseen, which transforms lives. . . ."

Jim launched his 1968 Easter sermon, "When the Stone Rolled," by almost setting the congregation rolling—in the aisles with laughter. It was actually a hard-hitting message on death and the Resurrection, but he softened up the audience first:

"Take heart. There is some good news in the news, and I thought I'd share it with you today. The Lauderdale Memorial Garden of Dreams is now planning a seventy-five-acre expansion in their cemetery which we are confidently told will make delightfully peaceful accommodiations for some 10,000 residents.

"And that's not the best part of it! In addition to this they are planning a thirty-five-story pure white marble mausoleum. Now isn't that thrilling? Think of the view! People are just dying to get in already!

"Imagine—the southeast exposure on the thirty-fifth floor! Just unbelievable! Don't rush down to buy it; it's already been purchased. The little bald-headed man who walked away with the contract was heard to mutter, 'Man, this is really living!' "

Jim went on to describe the great excitement in the news about heart transplants (it was 1968): "It's something that's a little hard for me to understand. Can you imagine some fellow saying, 'Darling, I love you with all of John's heart!'

"They even promise that in the very near future they're going to do away with heart disease altogether. Isn't that thrilling! Doesn't that just excite you? Nobody need ever die of heart failure again! Isn't it wonderful? Just think about it!

"We can all die of cancer . . . Yes sir-e-e-e, man, that's really living!"

In 1969 Jim preached a seven-part series on *Great Doctrines of Christianity.* The sermon on sanctification illustrates Jim's keen use of Latin and Greek, and the stress he places on correct doctrine:

"Christianity, indeed, is not only life, but it is also doctrine. It is a life which is produced by belief. Those who would castigate creed and dogma and doctrine should perchance take a look again at what these words mean.

"The word *doctrine* comes from the Latin word *docere,* which means *to teach.* The word *creed* comes from the Latin word *credo,* which means *I believe.* The word *dogma* comes from a Greek word *dokein* which means *to think.* Therefore, a person who has no dogma, no creed, and no doctrine is a person who neither teaches, believes, or thinks. If you're going to think anything, believe anything, and teach anything, then, my friends, you need dogma, creed, and doctrine. This is the substance which forms the foundation of the Christian faith."

Jim does not preach soothing sermons to lull comfortable pew-warmers into deeper somnolence.

"Do we say that the Church at large is filled more and more with unregenerate people who are no more than slightly veneered pagans who have come into the Church?" he asked the congregation one day. "How about you? Has your heart been transformed? Do you sit here every week, hypocritically, professing to be a Christian and knowing all the time that your life has never been changed, that you still lust after the things of the world? Do you know that you have not become a Christian? Are you still living in the same secret sins which only later shall be made manifest?

"We talk about the sanctification of the Church, but

what about the sanctification of the Church in your heart?"

Such direct, piercing proclamation apparently is too much for a few Coral Ridgers. In another sermon Kennedy told how one parishioner reacted to his preaching: "Someone came up to me at the door afterward and said, 'I quit this church.'

"The Bible says, 'Preach the Word for there will come a time when men will not endure sound doctrine but they will heap to themselves teachers having itching ears.' This is the problem today: too many people wanting their ears tickled.

"We need men who are willing to stand up and declare the Word of God regardless of the consequences. The Gospel of Jesus Christ has a cutting edge to it, my friend."

"I would like to ask you this," Kennedy demanded at the conclusion of his 1969 "State of the Church" sermon: "Where are you spiritually that you weren't a year ago at this time? What are you doing for Jesus Christ that you weren't doing a year ago?"

Few dare sidestep these questions.

9: REACHING OUT I:
INTO FORT LAUDERDALE

The Coral Ridge Presbyterian Church grew quite slowly at first. Then faster and faster.

Beginning in 1966, it was the fastest-growing congregation in the denomination. The Presbyterian Church in the U.S. has 960,000 members and 3,926 congregations (according to 1971 figures).

There is a direct connection between the Coral Ridge Church's growth and the number of its trained callers able to successfully make evangelism calls.

When the church was five years old there were only about thirty trained callers who went out regularly. Then Kennedy launched what he calls the "multi-stage rocket principle." This is simply the way those already trained are encouraged—even requested—to keep coming to successive training sessions. Each is asked to bring along two trainees. Thus you have an automatic program of enlargement—spiritual multiplication.

This plan keeps the evangelism rocket zooming toward target. "You don't do it in one big thrust," Jim advises. "You do it in stages. The important thing is not to lose momentum."

Church membership soon began to grow proportionately to the program success. During the past several years net membership increases have averaged about 350 persons annually. For six years it has been the fastest growing church in the Presbyterian Church in the United States.

Coral Ridge has led the denomination in professions of faith for six years. In 1970, for example, 180 persons joined the church by confessing their faith in Jesus Christ for the first time. The figure was 212 for 1969. (Only about .1 per cent of Presbyterian U.S. churches receive more than 100 members on profession of faith annually, according to statistics produced by church officials.) Hundreds of others have accepted Christ who could not become members because their homes are in the north.

Jim and his Coral Ridge staff are interested in much more than just adding numbers or compiling an impressive ecclesiastical body count. The quality and depth of commitment is far more important—both for the converts and for the vitality of the church.

One index to this concern for commitment is the number of persons devoting their lives to what is commonly called "full-time Christian service." This includes professional ministers, missionaries, and others whose vocations are directly related to preaching, teaching, or some form of evangelism.

Perhaps forty to fifty people at Coral Ridge indicated their desire to go into full-time service between the years 1966 and 1971, Jim estimates.

Eight or ten of these already were in their chosen field by mid 1971; another thirty were preparing.

At a recent missionary conference at the church, about a dozen young adults committed themselves to careers—either short- or long-term—on the mission field. Each of them had been won to Christ through some aspect of the Evangelism Explosion program.

Some of those young men and women are the products of chain-reaction witnessing that can be traced through several generations of Coral Ridge people.

As Jim says: "The spiritual children, grandchildren, and stepchildren produced by our people would probably count into the thousands."

Consider the case of Michael Wright, whose marriage ended in divorce when he was 26. Leaving his wife and child in Jacksonville, Florida, he took off for Miami. While he was standing at the side of the road, hitch-hiking, a car traveling at high speed smashed into his suitcase. The impact obliterated the bag and its contents.

Wright ended up in Miami with $50 in his wallet. The money was soon gone. He promptly landed—and lost—several jobs; he was unreliable, pilfered the stock, and dipped into the till.

After a few weeks he was broke, jobless—and desperate. Wright took a gun he had stolen from a bar and walked to a city park.

He sat down on a bench until he spotted a likely holdup victim: a small black man dressed in a business suit, seated on a park bench reading a book, a briefcase at his side. Sticking the gun muzzle in the man's ribs, Wright demanded: "Don't make a sound;

this is a stickup. Put everything in the briefcase and walk away and you won't get hurt."

The little Negro dropped the book he had been reading, jumped up, and reached his hand up to Wright's shoulder. "You can't hurt me unless God wants you to!" he exclaimed, looking Wright full in the face. "And besides, God loves you! What's more, I don't have any money. I'm a missionary. I run an orphanage in Haiti."

"Let me go!" stammered Mike. "Five hundred people in Bayfront Park and I have to stick up a missionary!"

Then, growing a little braver, he motioned the missionary to sit down again, and ordered him to stay there for five minutes until he could get away.

Wright fled—only to encounter the Haitian again just outside the park. Mike started to run.

"Michael," called Ernst, the black man, who says he doesn't know how he called him by his right name (Mike had not told him).

At this apparent supernatural phenomenon, Mike came completely unglued. He stopped in his tracks. Soon Ernst was witnessing to him. Among other things he told Mike he was going to be a flop as a crook if he could not pick better holdup prospects.

Finally he talked Mike into taking a bus with him to Fort Lauderdale. He gave him a name and an address. Before the two parted company, Ernst had led Michael to tearful repentance for his sins.

Michael threw away his gun!

He was on his way to a new life. The address was for

the home of Virginia Schmidt. In Coral Ridge circles she is better known as "Mama Bunny," the turned-on middle-aged woman who, with her husband, ministers to hundreds of seeking—and often problem-prone—young adults in the Fort Lauderdale community.

The Haitian missionary never pressed charges against Wright for the attempted holdup, but Mama Bunny did press the Gospel on his heart. Michael Wright fully accepted Christ as his Savior and began attending the Coral Ridge Church. Soon he decided he had better make up with his wife.

Mike got a job driving a laundry truck and began sending support payments to his wife in Jacksonville. He wrote Nancy he was sorry for the past and told her how God had changed his life.

Curious, Nancy came to Fort Lauderdale to see if he had blown his mind. The first night she was there, Virginia Schmidt explained to her what had happened to Mike. Of course, she also presented the Gospel to Nancy, who accepted Christ at 2:00 the next morning.

Mike moved Nancy and their child to Fort Lauderdale. He did not dare go back and live in Jacksonville: his father-in-law had sworn he would "shoot the guy" if he ever laid eyes on Mike again.

Mike and Nancy were remarried in the Coral Ridge Church by the Reverend Archie Parrish. A packed house of well-wishers looked on during the ceremony.

The Wrights' daughter was the flower girl.

Before long Nancy's mother, who hated Mike, heard that Mike and Nancy were reconciled. She, too, came to Fort Lauderdale, thinking Mike had conned Nancy with some kind of cruel joke just to get her back.

Nancy's mother was soon led to Christ. She immediately threw her arms around Mike and embraced him—something she had not done since shortly after her daughter's marriage to Mike Wright the first time.

Mike felt that God had restored their marriage for a definite purpose. Less than a year after he accepted Christ he enrolled at Belhaven College to prepare to become a minister of the Gospel.

How did Virginia Schmidt [Mama Bunny] become a Christian?

That story began with the impending breakup of a Miami couple. The wife's mother, who lived in Fort Lauderdale, told Jim Kennedy about her daughter's marriage problems. Jim helped untangle the snarls. In the process of counseling, the couple came to trust in Christ. Before long they moved to Fort Lauderdale.

The husband, at first very shy, became an avid Evangelism Explosion worker. He was instrumental in leading an elderly physician and his wife to the Lord shortly before the old man died.

A letter from the physician's widow spoke of the great joy she felt over her husband's acceptance of eternal life. "I have peace in my heart because I know where he is," wrote Mrs. Clifford Lancey.

That was not the only conversion precipitated by the Miami man who first saw Jim about his marriage problems. A retired army sergeant and his wife made commitments during another of his calls. That wife was Virginia Schmidt [Mama Bunny], herself now the spiritual mother of thousands. Within three months of the time she completed Evangelism Explosion training Virginia led thirty-nine persons to Christ.

Then there is the hygienist who worked for the Fort Lauderdale dentist, Dr. Freeman Springer. Freeman witnessed to her. Jim Kennedy also witnessed to her.

One day Jim was in the dental chair having his teeth cleaned. She confessed to him that she was about to break up a family: the man was going to leave his wife and children to marry her.

Jim didn't have a chance to say anything. His secretary called in the middle of the appointment to remind him about a funeral he was scheduled to conduct a few minutes later.

"Mama Bunny got hold of her and led her to Christ," Jim says, rounding out the story of the hygienist. It illustrates the way spiritual-family lines intersect and criss-cross through multiple witnessing.

Few testimonies are as moving as that of Dottie Springer, Freeman's wife. She has spoken to ministerial clinics at Coral Ridge.

As a young girl she was "very religious." She was president of her Christian Endeavor group.

As is true with many young people, though, her religious interest gradually cooled as she grew older. Years later, after visiting various churches with her husband, she said: "It wasn't like it used to be. They didn't preach out of the Bible; it was as if they were reading the Sunday paper."

Nevertheless, she and Freeman joined what she calls a "large, liberal church."

They climbed the Fort Lauderdale social ladder.

71

The Springers, who have four lovely daughters, acquired a large, expensive home. Dottie had two cars to use, furs, the whole bit. Life was a round of entertainment and self-indulgence: polo, races, cocktail parties, and nightclub dancing. Dottie Springer should have been one of the happiest women alive.

She wasn't. Like the song lyrics popularized by Peggy Lee, Dottie wondered, "Is that all there is?"

When she and Freeman heard Jim Kennedy give the invocation at an anti-Communism rally she began to think there was more.

When, at their request, Pastor Kennedy called in their home, she knew there was much more.

She wanted to know about going to the races, drinking, dancing. . . .

But after Jim asked her *the two questions,* the others did not really seem to matter.

Dottie, a tall, vivacious brunette, rededicated her life to Christ and started growing spiritually right away. Freeman entered into a personal relationship with Christ for the first time.

"This lay evangelism program," she told a crowd of ministers at the 1971 Coral Ridge clinic, "has meant everything in my life that is worthwhile and important."

"Christ became a reality," Dottie said softly to the attentive clergymen. "One of the most exciting days of my life was the first time I went out and shared with a friend who Jesus Christ really is and how you could know for certain that you are going to Heaven."

Dottie's friend received Christ.

Adds Dottie: "There's a joy that comes from sharing Christ that makes everything else seem dull and tarnished by comparison. . . . He put a song within my heart I had not known before.

Hollywood actor Chris Robinson also got more than he expected when he came into contact with Coral Ridge evangelism. He signed a contract to play Jim Kennedy in a fifty-five minute dramatic film titled *Like a Mighty Army*.

Gospel Films of Muskegon, Michigan, was casting the film, which tells the Evangelism Explosion story.

"I was and had been an agnostic most of my life," Robinson says by way of introduction to what happened to him. "In fact I was a very devout agnostic.

"I met Kennedy, auditioned, and got the part. As far as I was concerned, I was just going to play a role."

But getting to know Jim challenged his religious assumptions.

"It was the first time I heard a preacher who did not have just a blindly emotional presentation," Chris says.

Chris was introduced to "very interesting, exciting facts about Christianity and the Bible." He and Jim often lunched together and talked about spiritual matters.

Part of the film was shot at a small church in Wilton Manors near Fort Lauderdale. It stands at almost exactly the spot where Robinson was born.

The camera crews finished their work; but Chris, who maintains homes in Boynton Beach and Hollywood, California, continued to see Jim. They went sailing together. They had many long discussions that lasted until the wee hours. All the while the Holy Spirit was tenderizing Chris' heart.

Six to eight months passed.

One day Mrs. Robinson accepted Christ at the Kennedy home. Chris held out a couple of weeks longer, then he plunged. His life began to change.

He likes to think of the little church in Wilton Manors as the place where, in a sense, he was reborn some thirty years after his physical birth close by.

Chris did not immediately tell Jim he had invited Christ to rule his life.

The two went sailing one rough day. Chris blurted out that he had received Christ. Just then the boat nosedived in the surf.

"It was a dramatic explanation point to my statement," declares Chris.

10: REACHING OUT II: INTO ALL THE WORLD

The living flame of God's Word has passed from heart to heart, torched by evangelism, Coral Ridge style, from the tropics to the Arctic Circle.

Thousands of churches around the world are swinging into action, training laymen for witness in the Coral Ridge pattern. Kennedy's lectures, his popular book, the training films, and cassettes, and the renowned ministers' clinics at Fort Lauderdale and elsewhere have all played a part in bringing world attention to the Kennedy Evangelism Explosion.

Jim himself had told the Coral Ridge story to about 25,000 ministers and seminarians by the end of summer, 1971. Many of these lecture series—often six to ten hours in length—have been sponsored by the Billy Graham Evangelistic Association.

Jim has spoken to enthusiastic clergymen at numerous Crusade Schools of Evangelism; most are held in connection with Graham's major rallies. More than 550 ministers and seminary students, for example, heard Jim present the Evangelism Explosion plan during the Northern California Billy Graham Crusade at Oakland in July, 1971.

Some already were involved in the Coral Ridge program; others soon became participants.

The book *Evangelism Explosion* has enjoyed brisk sales at bookstores throughout the country (over 100,000 are in print). The 176-page volume tells how to train laymen for evangelism (this includes how to recruit and motivate participants and a complete sample run-through of the Gospel presentation; illustrations to use with the presentation; the proper use of testimony; how to handle objections; how to turn stumbling blocks into stepping stones; youth evangelism; and follow-up).

Charts and explanations are also included. Twenty-three memory verses are printed on card stock so they can be detached and—Navigator style—carried in a small holder for quick reference and easy memorization.

A companion item, *The Kennedy Cassettes on Lay Evangelism*, produced by David C. Cook Publishing Co., bring Dr. Kennedy's voice and explanations to you in his warm personal manner. The tapes are a companion to the book, *Evangelism Explosion* because they feature Dr. Kennedy's experience and know-how related to material in the book.

Gospel Films' runaway success, *Like a Mighty Army* is a fifty-five minute color documentary of the Coral Ridge story. The Muskegon, Michigan, firm reports it is the most popular rental film the company has produced in twenty years. *Like a Mighty Army* has also been produced with Spanish and Portuguese sound tracks.

Gospel Films points out that 51 percent of the churches renting *Like a Mighty Army* have started lay evangelism programs.

To assist these groups to implement the visitor training, Gospel Films later produced four more Coral Ridge movies. These instructional films, each twenty minutes long, are designed for churches and clinics and to be used in conjunction with the Kennedy books and cassette tapes.

The clinics at Fort Lauderdale have also propelled

the Kennedy method of personal evangelism to every part of the globe. During the first six years, ministers trekked to Fort Lauderdale from forty-eight states of the union, every province in Canada, and a dozen overseas countries.

When these ministers returned home—fired up about winning others—they became super-salesmen for personal lay evangelism. Clergymen from Japan, Korea, Australia, England, Germany, New Zealand, and South Africa have imported it.

Many have started not only programs, but ministers' clinics of their own. Jim estimates between thirty and forty churches have had their own clinics for ministers; some have held two or more.

Jim himself has instructed pastors and/or held brief clinics in Canada, Switzerland, Guatemala, and the Bahamas. He is scheduled to address a ministerial gathering of all the pastors in Taiwan in the spring of 1972.

Hundreds of ministers and missionaries from the United States and abroad have caught a new vision for training their people in "doing the work of ministry" (Ephesians 4).

Not everyone who would like to come to the February Fort Lauderdale clinics can be accepted. Accommodations in homes are one limitation. Also, Jim wants to make sure every pastor will have a trained lay partner from Coral Ridge to take him out on calls.

In February, 1971, for instance, 250 ministers from thirty states and a number of foreign countries came to Fort Lauderdale for the church's sixth annual evangelism clinic. Another 1500 were turned away.

Several of the ministers who came to Coral Ridge to learn evangelism techniques, found that revival had to begin close to home. With them, in fact.

Jim notes several conversions among the clergy,

including the head of evangelism for one denomination.

A few of the ministers keep coming back to attend a second, or even third, clinic. They are encouraged to share with those attending for the first time how the Coral Ridge plan has worked in their own church or community.

Many of these testimonies have been taped for other training meetings.

"Listening to tapes of how churches have been utterly transformed is one of the greatest thrills and challenges I know," declares Kennedy.

There are many thrilling episodes.

Perhaps no other clergyman had done more to implement the Coral Ridge plan on a worldwide scale than the Reverend Robert F. Armstrong.

Armstrong, who has attended all but the first of the six Coral Ridge ministers' clinics, is pastor of the Warrendale Community Church in suburban Detroit. His congregation is extremely missionary-minded: it supports seventy-seven missionaries. Armstrong also has a weekday radio ministry on WMUZ-FM each morning and evening.

The church, originally a Presbyterian mission, became independent in 1950. It has been singled out for particular honors. In 1970 it was chosen number one in the Class A Division of the National Sunday School Association, an honor topping the "Church of the Year" award three years in a row by the Michigan Sunday School Association.

Armstrong first heard of Kennedy through his wife, when Mrs. Armstrong heard a tape about Coral Ridge at a meeting. Armstrong, 46 and white-haired, enrolled in the 1967 clinic. It revolutionized his entire ministry.

Armstrong and his assistant pastor have held their own evangelism clinics all over the United States and overseas. One hundred sixty laymen from Warrendale have been trained in Coral Ridge outreach.

Armstrong ties the steady growth in the church (about 15 per cent each year) to the advent of Evangelism Explosion. The church needs ten more acres for expansion, Bob says, despite the fact that a $500,000 addition was recently completed.

Six hundred parishioners are enrolled in Bible study classes three nights a week.

Further, staff members of twenty-five churches in the greater Detroit area have been trained in evangelism through Warrendale's outreach.

In mid-1971 Armstrong led a dozen from his congregation in a clinic in Jamaica. Before that, twenty parishioners joined him in a highly successful three-day clinic in Chatham, Ontario, Canada. Eighty persons professed faith in Christ.

In November of 1970 Armstrong held a mass rally for ministers in Toronto. He has shared the Coral Ridge plan in Belgium, Holland, Rome, Jaipur, Pakistan, and Kodiak, Alaska.

Warrendale has a separate teen-age training program on Sunday afternoons, collegian teams go out witnessing, and Warrendale-sponsored full-time workers in Kenya and at Chicago's Moody Bible Institute are engaged in Evangelism Explosion techniques. A daughter clinic at Warrendale attracts forty to fifty ministers annually.

Armstrong has carried out his ministry in about forty countries; Bible conference work is his specialty. In the summer of 1971 he was working out details for a team to share the Coral Ridge program in Kenya, Africa.

In a letter outlining more projected outreach he wrote:

"We will be sharing the program in the coming months in a rally with the Independent Fundamental Churches of America (IFCA); in the St. Catherine, Ontario, region with the Mennonite denomination in October, and in Toronto, Ontario, Canada, in November.

"I can enthusiastically recommend the Coral Ridge evangelism program that Dr. D. James Kennedy taught us as the answer to the spiritual growth in our church."

Canadian pastor John Moran of Toronto's Parkway Bible Church could not agree more.

Moran, who has directed three daughter clinics, added 103 members to his church during the first eight months after he instituted the Coral Ridge program there.

A granddaughter outreach stretched all the way to a community of Eskimos in an Arctic town on Baffin Island.

Moran first heard of the Coral Ridge program through his brother, Leslie Moran, a Presbyterian Church, U.S., clergyman who knew Kennedy.

It was natural that the Morans, when vacationing in Fort Lauderdale, should visit Coral Ridge. Moran was impressed.

He attended the February, 1969, ministers' clinic. When he returned to Parkway Church (affiliated with the Associated Gospel Churches), he began a modest training program with three teams of two persons each.

There were decisions for Christ the first night; "That set the spiritual tone," Moran recalls.

Soon ten visitors were making calls. "That," he adds, "was the greatest thrill of my thirty years in the ministry." Two years later, he had forty trained visitors.

During a report session at a clinic, held at Ontario Bible College, a Pentecostal minister stood to give a testimony. The pastor of Scarborough Gospel Temple, Toronto, he had attended an earlier Moran clinic at Parkway. As a result he took a team of young people from his church to Baffin Island. There they visited practically every home in a small Arctic town.

He told the astonished Toronto audience that fifty Eskimos made decisions for Christ.

Moran sums up the excitement that has spread from the tropics to the Arctic hinterland: "The whole thrill of this is that we have seen growth and seen people become soul winners. They are doing something they never thought they could."

The Coral Ridge outreach has also permeated entire denominations.

The Associate Reformed Presbyterian Church (28,-000 members) and the Reformed Presbyterian Evangelical Synod (14,000 members) have designated the Coral Ridge plan as the official or model evangelism program for their denominations.

The American Lutheran Church (2.5 million members), while not officially endorsing the Coral Ridge approach as its own, has hundreds of participating congregations.

The Reverend E. H. Schalkhauser, the American Lutheran Church associate director of evangelism, says his department makes the Coral Ridge plan available as "one of the ways" effective evangelism can be carried out successfully in the local church.

Perhaps no church is more involved with the Coral Ridge program than the 2.8 million-member Lutheran Church-Missouri Synod.

The Reverend Theodore Raedeke, former evangelism head of the denomination, was unstinting in his praise when asked about the success of Kennedy's Evangelism Explosion among Lutheran Church-Missouri Synod churches.

"I think it's the answer for in-depth evangelism training," says Raedeke, who has also recommended Evangelism Explosion as a resource and training tool for the trans-denominational evangelism effort, Key 73.

A letter from the Reverend Gerald Schultz of Detroit to the Reverend Archie Parrish, Coral Ridge's minister of evangelism, underscores Raedeke's observations:

"A little over two years have passed since our first contact with your program, and I think I'm safe in saying that more practical evangelism has been taking place in Michigan during these two years than in the total eighty-nine-year history of our District. (Our district involves 327 congregations with 173,000 members.)

"Perhaps the most valuable result has been the clinics which were provided by the Reverend Jerrold Nichols at Bethlehem Lutheran of Saginaw where 225 pastors have had field training under laymen who have been active in the Kennedy technique. . . .

"I have conducted a total of twenty of the lay clinics and have had over 2,500 lay people enrolled. Some of these were made up exclusively of elders who were directed toward inreach evangelism, aimed at the uncommitted who were still on the church records.

"I have also run clinics in nine other states, using the Coral Ridge outline, but without running the trainees through the observation process of field calls. One of the most exciting involved 150 young people at Lake Okoboji, Iowa.

"A new door has just opened among a Christian women's organization of our church which has traditionally been devoted to missions and evangelism. This group, the Lutheran Women's Missionary League, has now scheduled seven clinics during their weekend retreats in various areas of Michigan. They are an extremely receptive group!

"Our latest venture involves the contracting of Professor Richard Korthals of Concordia Lutheran College of Ann Arbor to develop the Coral Ridge program in individual congregations of Michigan. We are most anxious for him to attend your clinic this coming September. . . . (A mini-clinic, the first of its type, was held at Coral Ridge September 11-15, 1971. About twenty ministers and church workers were invited.)

"It is not difficult to see from all this that we owe even more to our Lord Jesus whose hand of blessings seems to turn everything we touch to *spiritual gold!*"

11: PEOPLE WANT TO KNOW . . .

"Yeah, well . . . that's nice—but. . . ."

"*What about me?* I get nervous when I see a stranger. I'm shy, and I could never call on people I don't know!"

Jim Kennedy was shy, too. So was his wife. Anne still wonders how she will be received when she knocks on a door.

Look at how the Lord has used them!

"When people say 'I'm not cut out for this,' I say 'hogwash!' " exudes Kennedy. "You are exactly the type of person for whom we've designed this program. I want you to come and learn and listen at the seminars."

Those who do and who stick with it gain a knowledge of the Bible. That gives them confidence. Soon they forget their fears.

That is the way those with objections to the Coral Ridge program usually begin their criticisms or voice their doubts, says Jim Kennedy.

Archie Parrish, the Coral Ridge Presbyterian minister of evangelism who has made a tremendous contribution to the development of the program, has a fat file full of letters from people around the world seeking advice and information about the plan.

People want to know such things as: *"Where do you get prospects?" "How do you get those who have made decisions, to come to church?" "How do you get people to take part in the training program?" "How do you keep them coming back year after year?" "What if they are already too busy with other things?" "How many (or what percentage) of those who make professions continue in the faith?" "How does the program affect giving to the church?" "What about follow-up?"*

Critical questions and outright criticism of the Coral Ridge plan can be divided—in general—into two types of comments: those made by persons who believe in personal evangelism but find difficulty with the Coral Ridge program; and those made by persons who disavow personal evangelism altogether.

From the latter camp, Kennedy gets questions such as: "What church-school curriculum do you use at Coral Ridge?" "What are you doing to reach black people?" is another interrogation.

Parrish has prepared answers to many of the common questions that seek information or ask, "How do you ...?"

Kennedy's book, *Evangelism Explosion,* details answers to some of the questions too. For example, it points out (page 13) that the best sources of prospects are: (1) People who have visited worship services; (2) Parents of children enrolled in the church school; (3) Community service or Chamber of Commerce listings of new area residents; and (4) a house-to-house religious survey and opinion poll leading into a presentation of the Gospel.

Answers to other questions may be found on the tapes, *Kennedy Cassettes on Lay Evangelism,* available for Coral Ridge-type training clinics or personal use.

Frequently a questioner will pose this omnibus query: *"What does Evangelism Explosion program do to the total life of a church?"*

In 1970, the Reverend Robert Armstrong of Warrendale Community Church in suburban Detroit held a clinic at Barcroft Bible Church in Arlington, Virginia.

Eighteen months later (September, 1971), Barcroft's pastor, the Reverend Marlin C. Hardman, reported this about Evangelism Explosion in his thriving, metropolitan Washington, D.C., congregation:

"More people are coming to know Christ than ever before. Our services have never been better attended. One of the reasons is our Coral Ridge program. It has transformed my ministry. The first six months there were six of us [trained workers]; the second six months, eighteen of us. Next month there will be forty-two."

Here are the words of a United Presbyterian minister, the Reverend Robert Whitaker, associate pastor of the First Presbyterian Church of Glendale, California:

"I tried it tentatively, and then on a little larger scale. After training ten people in the program, and visiting quite a number of people, I find it's the most effective evangelism tool that I've ever used in my ministry.

"God is blessing it and using it, and we've had a remarkable response. Out of the first fifty people that we called on, about 50 per cent received Christ as Lord and Savior."

Do the conversions last?

Of course there are dropouts. There are in every form of evangelism. Those interviewed attest to what they consider a high percentage of "stickers" who still keep the faith years after their act of commitment to Christ.

What about follow-up?

Coral Ridge works hard on its follow-up ministry. There are study materials that lay evangelists leave after a person makes a commitment, and when the evangelist makes the follow-up call the following week. A new and exciting cassette follow-up ministry has been developed. Individual and group return visits are made. Converts are channeled into Bible studies for new Christians. Callers are given extensive training in how to make follow-up calls on those they reach through the program.

New members of the church are instructed, then integrated into the total life of the congregation. Mature in the faith church members sponsor one or more of the new members. Follow-up at Coral Ridge is so important that the Reverend James C. Bland is assigned to it full time.

For those who want to learn more about Coral Ridge follow-up, *Evangelism Explosion* describes the step-by-step procedures and forms that work in Fort Lauderdale.

Others cross-examine Kennedy about how the church stands on social action. *"What are you doing to change the social structures?"* they ask.

Jim's answer is prompt and unequivocal: Society is changed through the Gospel. Indirectly rather than directly. As he sees it, the mission of the Church is "to change the hearts and minds of people who will then have an impact on society." Many of the people of Coral Ridge are already having quite an impact on their city.

According to many testimonies on tape and in letters possessed by Archie Parrish, converted people do just that, not only in Fort Lauderdale, but around the country.

The associate pastor of a United Presbyterian church in Cincinnati, Ohio, wrote Archie about "a real balance" in his church between personal evangelism and social action. He said this was a result of the Coral Ridge program.

The church now has a project to train the unemployed, outreach ministries to young people with drug problems, and a ministry to poor people in the community.

"The layman learns quickly," the minister wrote, "that concern for personal salvation loses authenticity if it is not linked with a genuine compassion for human suffering in this world."

The doubt about the Coral Ridge plan probably raised the most often is: *"Isn't this approach too 'canned,' too mechanical?"*

That is exactly what Bob Whitaker of Glendale,

California, thought. So did the Reverend Robert M. Christiansen, another United Presbyterian clergyman.

Christiansen, pastor of Concord, California's, First Presbyterian Church for more than eleven years, felt queasy about the Coral Ridge presentation. He thought it was too rigid.

Not long after he attended an Evangelism Explosion clinic he was asked to call on a 35-year-old man thought to be dying of a communicable disease. The man was not a Christian. His wife and mother had been praying for him.

Bob Christiansen donned a hospital gown and mask. He was permitted to visit the patient in his isolated room for only five minutes.

Immediately the critically ill man asked: "How can I know about eternal life?"

Christiansen used the five-point Gospel presentation he had learned at the Cincinnati clinic and led the man to Christ. It was a genuine conversion. What's more, the man was amazingly healed. Today he leads a vibrant Christian life.

Christiansen no longer doubts the efficacy of a simple Gospel outline and presentation.

Many, whose first reactions were that the program is too mechanical, have tried it and changed their minds. The merits of any evangelism program can be judged only after a fair trial.

Also near the top on the criticism list is: *"The Coral Ridge approach won't work in our area"*; or, *"It won't work with our people."*

Naturally not every church will have the same

measure of success Fort Lauderdale has had. Fort Lauderdale, with a population of 200,000—and another 200,000 transients during the winter—is ideally suited for Evangelism Explosion.

A small town of 2,700 might soon be saturated by a large calling force. Nonetheless, Evangelism Explosion techniques have been used successfully in hamlets and in large cities, with Eskimos and with sophisticated seminarians.

The crux of the matter, says Jim Kennedy, is that, when adapted as needed, the Evangelism Explosion plan can produce spiritual fruit in any situation. He is convinced it can win and hold more persons for Christ in any given geographical area than if the plan were not used. "There will be greater results whatever the situation you're in," he says.

Few skeptics want to wager against that.

12: THE CORAL RIDGE EXPLOSION

The present Coral Ridge church was selected in 1970 by *Decision* magazine as one of five outstanding churches in North America.

The secret of Coral Ridge Presbyterian is that it teaches its members how to share Jesus Christ with others. Not many churches—unfortunately—can make that statement.

Just as Jim Kennedy made an unspectacular start as Coral Ridge's pastor, so the church itself had an obscure beginning. The first service was held in McNab school on May 3, 1959. Groundbreaking for the first sanctuary was held on Sunday, October 8, 1961, at 50th Street and 18th Terrace, an area that had come to be known as "Larson's Folly."

(At that time the site was a sight, all right. Out in the boondocks north of town, it was little more than shifting sand, high weeds, and a scattering of palm trees.)

Larson, a presbytery executive, was a man of vision—not foolishness, however, and the area grew. By 1964 an education wing was added. Twelve additional lots were acquired in September of 1965 including the land on which a fire station stands.

91

The fire house, adjacent to the sanctuary, blocked the church's expansion in that direction. In an imaginative move, Coral Ridge Church agreed to build a new fire house on church-owned land on the other side of the sanctuary in exchange for the old fire house and lot. Thus contiguous property totaling six acres was negotiated.

The old fire house was converted into a Teen Tower and a day school for preschoolers. Church offices were put upstairs. Coral Ridge became one of the safest places for persons who fear fire: a church that offers "fire insurance" situated between two fire stations!

By May, 1968, when the church had grown to 1,366 members, plans were well under way to vastly expand on the six-acre site. The Sunday-school wing, already serving about 800 children and youth in double sessions, was especially cramped.

The idea: Plan for the expanded facilities one year—including raising the money—and occupy the new plant the following year.

It did not work out that way. Planning took nearly two years. By that time, church growth had run away from the plans; the six-acre site was already too small for the church family.

Back to the drawing board!

"The church has run off several times and we have come running after it," says Jim Kennedy. "Like the parents of a runaway child, we have to run after him to find out how to treat him."

Can a church get too big and unwieldy? Perhaps, Jim thinks. In his view, any church that is larger than two or three hundred members has the problem of bigness. Many of the members know one another only superficially—if at all.

That is why Jim has concentrated on creating a variety of smaller groups within the church. Special care is given to "garnering new members" and assimilating them gradually into the work and witness of the congregation. Coral Ridge has forty to fifty Bible-study groups in progress all year.

"People have the idea that an evangelistic church is shallow in every other way," Jim observes. "We have felt it is important to have a well-rounded church that includes evangelism, worship, education, fellowship, missions, and other aspects of church life."

He adds that a big church can do things a small one can't "if you really work at it."

Coral Ridge really works at providing the diversified spiritual menu Jim holds up as the ideal.

During much of the year there are three Sunday morning worship services and one on Sunday nights. Experienced ushers, wearing white coats with red carnations in the lapels, glide efficiently down the aisles. They seat capacity crowds of 800 at most morning services. Music director Roger McMurrin and organist Diane Bish lead a blue-robed choir of 95 in stirring anthems and pace the congregation in singing hymns from *The Worship and Service Hymnal*.

Anne Kennedy, who sings in the choir, keeps her eyes raptly fixed on Jim. Draped in a royal blue gown, he steps into the pulpit. An expectant hush settles over the congregation as he begins to preach. Most people in the audience follow his text in their own Bibles.

Sunday evening services are less formal. There is special music—a solo, trio, or perhaps an instrumental group. Usually someone who has something to share—and has prepared it ahead of time—gives a five-minute testimony. Hundreds of personal testimonies by persons reached through the Coral Ridge ministry are recorded on tape and filed—along with an equal number of Jim's sermons—in the church's well-equipped tape library.

Between morning services—8:15, 9:30 and 11:00—parishioners mingle in the crowded narthex and patio, exchanging greetings and—more likely than not—discussing spiritual concerns.

There is an esprit de corps at Coral Ridge that even a casual visitor can feel. Though this is an intangible, it is exemplified by the illuminated auto tags Coral Ridgers bolt on their cars. Florida does not issue plates for the front bumpers, and many residents install their own tags displaying monograms, emblems, or slogans.

The Coral Ridge tag is a blue fish emblem with the Greek word "ICHTHUS" on it. Meaning "fish," the word is an early Christian symbol and an acrostic for Jesus Christ, God's Son, Savior. Church members, spotting the tags any where in town, honk and wave to one another.

Coral Ridge offers the typical large-church plethora of Sunday and weekday activities for all ages. There are seven choirs, and a chancel choir/church orchestra of 150 was forming in the fall of 1971.

There is a lively group for single young adults. That class and one for couples must meet across the street on Sundays in unused rooms of Holy Cross Hospital because of overcrowding at the church. Another singles group called the "39ers" is for those "thirty-nine and holding."

Women's circles number sixteen. There are a unit of Pioneer Girls and a battalion of Boys' Brigade. A Spiritual Fitness Program, divided into small groups, meets in homes weekly.

The Midweek School of the Bible, taught by the Coral Ridge staff, offers adult electives as well as classes for youth and children. A turnout of 400 at the Wednesday night program is not unusual.

For the fall, 1971, quarter, the Midweek School offered: Christian Doctrine, a systematic study of Biblical theology, taught by Jim Kennedy; Basic Family Conflicts, a new approach to living, by minister to youth Sim Fulcher; Life Changing Conversations With Jesus, led by William Swets, minister of pastoral care; Can You Separate the Christian Church and Music? by music director Roger McMurrin; Bible Survey (Genesis through Esther for the quarter), led by Archie Parrish; and a course in practical Christian living, The Joy of Discovery, taught by the minister of follow-up, James Bland. Courses in New Testament Greek have also been taught.

Other full-time ministerial and administrative staff at the church include the Reverend Sherwood Strodel, minister of education; the Reverend Robert Koren, extension minister; the Reverend Harry Miller—serving on the Coral Ridge staff for the second time, currently as headmaster of the new private school, Westminster Academy which includes pre-school through high school; and George Johnston, executive administrator.

There are also twenty-five secretarial, administrative, and custodial employees plus 27 teachers at Westminster Academy.

How much money does it take to run such a Gospel-disseminating industry? The 1971 budget was $830,000 for operating costs and $147,000 for missions. Twenty missionaries are wholly or partially supported by Coral Ridge. The budget for 1972 will be well over a million dollars. The church is aiming at a million dollars a year in benevolences in a few years.

The church's youth work, capably led by 35-year-old Sim Fulcher, who has been at Coral Ridge since 1964, is essential to congregational vitality. Some 250 junior high, high school, and college-age young people are active each week; about twenty volunteer youth counselors and advisors work with them. The Teen Tower youth lounge (located where fire trucks used to be) is open four days a week for recreation, spiritual training, and as an outreach ministry for hundreds of young people.

Sim Fulcher says the weekend conference approach has emerged as the heart of the Coral Ridge youth program. Hundreds of young people of all ages take part in monthly campouts and overnight conferences.

"These provide a kind of soak time," Sim says, "a

time when kids come to know Christ firsthand and develop a working, personal, live relationship to Him."

A sizable group of the older young people participate in a youth division of Evangelism Explosion, and Sim is reorganizing the senior high department (eleventh and twelfth graders) to be a leadership training program and service corps instead of strictly a "youth group."

When peak church attendance on several Sundays between Christmas and Easter hit 2,850, it became obvious that the 50th Street facility—even with careful site development—could not possibly provide enough room for the future.

A new site of 15.2 acres—the land alone is already worth $2 million—was secured a few blocks away. A new 2500 seat sanctuary will be completed by, Christmas, 1972. The entire new complex will be completed, hopefully by 1975. The present facility has been sold to another church.

The switch occasioned a planning delay of at least two years. In 1971 (at last!) the new sanctuary and tower started to rise. Westminster Academy, with thirty large rooms for classes was completed.

The new church complex (exclusive of the academy) will cost at least $6 million. The site on Federal Highway 1 in north Fort Lauderdale, bounded by apartment houses and a Ramada Inn, will soon be dominated by a 300-foot tower with foundations rooted forty feet deep. The new sanctuary will seat 2,500; 5,000 children and adults can be accommodated in double-session Sunday school classes when the total complex, including Westminster Academy, is complete.

The tower and steeple, with faceted glass on all four sides, will lift the cross of Christ high over the surrounding landscape and be visible for miles in all directions. A carillon will waft hymns from the top of the tower.

A cascading fountain, depicting the Water of Life, will stand immediately in front of the tower entrance.

Westminster Academy, the new school, is a kind of ninety-day wonder. On March 13, 1971, the Coral Ridge Church session decided there was a need for the school as an agency of the church. (The church had been involved with other churches in a Christian school for four years, but now felt that the time had come to establish their own school.)

Money was raised, headmaster Harry Miller and twenty teachers were hired, and the building was well under construction—all in a few weeks. Westminster opened September 1.

"The whole thing has been built through prayer, love, and Christian unity. All the teachers have really pulled together," beams Nora Day, effervescent Westminster booster and school secretary.

Jim Kennedy believes a key to the church's success on so many fronts is the congregation's corporate prayer life. For the last few years Coral Ridge has launched the calendar year with a week of prayer. The officers and another 300 or so Coral Ridgers faithfully assemble at the church from 5 to 7 each morning for two hours of prayer and to establish goals for the coming year.

The church, notes Kennedy, became the fastest-growing congregation in the denomination the same year it started this practice. (It has had this distinction now for six years.) He believes this is no coincidence.

Professor Richard Korthals of Concordia Lutheran College at Ann Arbor said the same thing in a different idiom. In Fort Lauderdale to attend a fall mini-clinic before promoting Evangelism Explosion among Lutheran Church-Missouri Synod congregations in Michigan, Korthals gave an impromptu testimony to a banquet crowd of 318 assembled at the Galt Ocean Mile Hotel to kick off the clinic:

"To really do the job, an explosion has to begin down underneath, on the bottom—not on the top. The Coral Ridge Explosion started underneath. That's why it's so successful."

13: MAMA BUNNY'S GREENHOUSE

Virginia Schmidt had not been a Christian very long before she was tagged with the nickname, "Mama Bunny." The "Tuesday Night Thing" that met in the Schmidts' Fort Lauderdale home was dubbed "the Bunny Club."

It all started because Virginia was such a prodigious evangelist for Christ. Freeman Springer's hygienist, Barbara, one of the first converts brought to Christ through Virginia, was joking with Jim one day about all the spiritual offspring Virgina was producing.

"Why, she's a regular spiritual rabbit!" Barbara chuckled.

"Yeah," shot back Jim, "that's Mama Bunny!"

The name stuck. So has Rene [Virginia's husband] and Virginia Schmidts' love for Christ and for introducing others to Him.

Virginia, a warm, humble lady of charm and Christlike concern, felt "a compelling pull into learning how to share the Gospel in spite of herself . . . a hypnotic, irresistible force." Like many other Coral Ridgers, she thought witnessing required a special ability she did not have.

Virginia was driven by that force: there had been nothing in her life before or has not been since that she has wanted to do more, Virginia told a friend one sultry summer day about seven years after she first gave her heart to Christ.

100

Not long after that commitment, she and her husband, Rene, learned how to present the Gospel at a witnessing session (in 1966). Once she had some basic training in presenting the Gospel, Virginia became a witnessing fireball—with a velvet touch.

Even repairmen, summoned to the Schmidts' house to service ailing appliances, came to know Christ through Virginia's presentation.

It got to the point that Virginia and Rene prayed: "Lord, let anything break down so that we might win more to Christ—as long as we have the money to get it fixed."

That is the kind of Christians the Schmidts are.

Early in 1970 the Schmidts' only son, Danny, 25, was tragically killed in a motorcycle accident. A 62-year-old Fort Lauderdale woman, thinking an intersection was clear, accidentally plowed into young Schmidt's cycle. He died six hours after surgeons futilely struggled to patch up his crushed body on the operating table. Virginia had led her son to Christ only three years before. . . .

A week after Danny's funeral, Virginia called on the remorseful woman motorist and led her to the Lord. A Catholic, the woman came to the Coral Ridge Church the next Wednesday evening with Virginia. With strong emotion and overflowing heart, she prayed aloud during the service, thanking God for his forgiveness and for Virginia's amazing love.

There was hardly a dry eye in the house.

"The Bunny Club," as it is sometimes jokingly referred to, began in March of 1969. The Schmidts' daughter, Lucinda, was away at school in Miami. A young girl named Livia from Rio de Janeiro needed a place to stay. Having an extra bedroom, the Schmidts agreed to take her until she found a permanent home.

Virginia says she felt an instant love for the pretty

101

South American senorita. Livia, in turn, had an instant liking for Virginia, and an immediate hunger for the Lord. Within hours of her arrival at the Schmidts she had made a solid commitment to Christ.

Livia wanted to share her experience right away with the other foreign students in the English class she was attending, so she asked Virginia if she could bring them to the Schmidt home to hear about the Lord and the Bible.

One Tuesday night in March, 1969, eight or ten of Livia's friends came to a potluck dinner at the Schmidts. The evening was a smashing success. They all came back a week later.

That time they brought *their* friends. "We haven't missed a Tuesday night since," declares Virginia.

Other young adults in the 18-30 age range were often around the house. Some were spiritual children of the Schmidts; others sought spiritual counseling. Many, both single and married, just seemed to gravitate to the warm cheeriness of the Schmidt household.

About that time Glenda Delmar, the pert, new director of Christian education for Coral Ridge Church, came to town. She, too, was often at the Schmidt home.

Within just a few weeks the Tuesday Night Thing mushroomed to forty or fifty people. Soon the Schmidts had to buy a larger house to accommodate all the eager young people—longhairs and straights, singles and marrieds.

Rene, an engineering inspector with the city of Fort Lauderdale, figured the new house at 161 NW 36th Street could handle about seventy-five to eighty kids. What he didn't figure on was the snowballing crowds.

Soon spiritually hungry kids were jamming the

living and dining rooms and four bedrooms to capacity.

"Why, there were kids peering around the bathroom corner, out on the patio, and even in the swimming pool—when it was empty," laughs Virginia.

When the Tuesday Night Thing hit 200, Rene and Virginia started another Tuesday Night Thing—on Monday nights. That, too, grew. Some of the Tuesday gang came, but it was largely a new batch of young people who attended.

By that time the Schmidt home and its program were becoming widely known. Guests from age three to eighty-four dropped in or were brought by the regulars. One night even the Oakland Park police, responding to a hot tip, rolled up to investigate.

An anonymous caller had informed them that a huge pot party was in progress. When the patrol car pulled up, the officers found cars parked for blocks around and in every available vacant lot. They did not hear a sound from the house.

"What's going on?" one demanded of Rene Schmidt, who was out in the driveway directing traffic. (Rene, the logistics arm of the operation, had been spending two nights a week in his driveway for the better part of two years. He even ate his dinner out there.)

Rene motioned the patrolman to a side window. The cop's eyes popped. There, sure enough, were scores of young people, jammed into every corner and cranny. Many wore long hair and beards; all were casually dressed. There was no marijuana. Not even a plain cigarette was in sight. These young people had Bibles on their laps, and they were listening to the speaker. It happened to be Jim Kennedy talking about Satan!

Early in its development, the Schmidt outreach program came to be known as the Greenhouse. The name means something to Christians—the place where spiritual growth sprouts. Yet it isn't overtly religious —that might turn off non-Christians. Part of the genius of the Greenhouse is its non-churchy approach. Ninety per cent of the young people would never come if the meetings were held in church.

From the beginning, the Tuesday—and then Monday—night meetings have been built around food and fellowship. "It's a bring what you can arrangement," says Virginia. Eager eaters always find plenty of good, hot food to chow down.

The incidentals and extra food items that always seem to be needed cost money. Until early 1971 the Schmidts picked up the tab for all this. More recently, circles from the church women's group provided help with the meals.

The physical food is all prelude to the spiritual fare that is regularly dished up.

"Our goal was to lead new Christians into the Bible," Virginia explained to a visitor, "but this became immediately evangelistic."

Virginia, and Glenda Delmar were the initial teachers. They used a variety of Bible study techniques, breaking the crowd into small groups to study selected verses of Scripture. Interest blossomed—and so did the young people's esteem for Mama Bunny.

She and Glenda, who later resigned her job as Director of Christian Education to devote full time to the Greenhouse ministry, make sure the crowd has a good time while Christ and God's Word are exalted. That way the Christian young people have no qualms about inviting unsaved friends.

It is not unusual to record twenty new professions of faith every week.

As the two groups Virginia and Glenda taught hit the 100 to 200 attendance mark, four classes were set up, each with a different teacher. This was expanded to six groups, with one, called "the Way," reserved for all newcomers. First-time attenders are assigned to that class whether or not they have previously professed faith in Christ.

New converts are next eased with tender care from this class to a five-week series on basics of the faith ("the Truth"). Other electives, lasting six weeks, are offered for the more mature in the faith ("the Life").

Even this two-night program was not enough: soon a third night had to be set up. In response to demand, Bunny and Glenda teach a Friday night course on Biblical psychology to forty to fifty young people. More than a few regulars now attend seminary or plan to follow mission careers. Many have found their way into active service in Coral Ridge Presbyterian and other local congregations.

At least half a dozen counselors assist the Schmidts and Glenda, who give personal attention to the dozens of young people who often drop by or phone at any hour of the day or night.

Still, the job has been taxing. The sheer volume of bodies and automobiles caused frayed nerves around the neighborhood despite Rene's gerrymandering of cars and polished PR efforts.

Finally, bone tired, Rene and Virginia closed their home for the month of August, 1971, and left for a much-needed vacation—their first in several years. They had the carpets professionally cleaned while they were gone. (Virginia notes that the total damage to their home after two and a half years of twice-and-thrice-weekly sieges by animated youths is a cigarette burn in one chair.)

You do not shut down something like the Greenhouse, though. It just won't quit. When the Schmidts returned from vacation there were high hopes that a vacant private school, with ample space and an inviting atmosphere, could be purchased as the Greenhouse's future home. Dedicated laymen had already pledged $100,000.

"We feel God wants a new, larger Greenhouse," said Virginia with characteristic unwavering faith. And her prayer for 1972: 500 disciples, nurtured in the Greenhouse and transplanted into the world to serve Christ.

Judging from its amazing beginning, the Greenhouse will produce a bumper crop. Revolutionaries, drug addicts, kids with serious home problems—all have found help at Mama Bunny's. They have found someone who cares—and who introduces them to the Someone who can change them completely. This is an example of the social effects of evangelism on the community.

Virginia Schmidt is careful about the credit for all that is happening: "None of us as human beings had anything in the world to do with it," she insists. "It's the Holy Spirit using our availability."

Tom Hanna, 40, but boyish-looking, agrees with that statement 100 per cent. He was a counselor-worker at the Greenhouse until he started another Coral Ridge spinoff ministry in the spring of 1971. It is as unique and blessed by the Lord as Mama Bunny's Greenhouse, though the focus and approach are far different.

"The rattier they look, the more open they seem to be . . . Jesus Christ is not an offense," Tom said, describing the nightly street-scraping technique he and his workers use at His Place, a beach ministry to hippies along Fort Lauderdale's famed strip. (There is no connection to the His Place in Hollywood, California, operated by hip minister Arthur Blessitt.)

The coffeehouse beach ministry just exploded when a Christian businessman in the Coral Ridge church made the lobby and several rooms of his beachside

106

motel available to Tom during the resort's off season —and another Coral Ridger paid the $100-a-month rent for the place.

"During Easter Week, Campus Crusade, Inter-Varsity, Youth for Christ, and a bunch of other evangelical groups came in droves to Fort Lauderdale to witness," Tom recalls. When they moved on, there was not any permanent ministry to the hordes of hippies— and some "weekend hippie-types"—who congregate along the nightclub-and-pizza-house dotted highway known as the strip.

Tom, who came to Christ at the age of 18 through a Youth for Christ Club in Hawaii, has been active in the Coral Ridge Church for years. An elder, he was teaching an adult class as well as counseling at the Greenhouse. Still, he felt restless. As an ordained minister (Unevangelized Fields Mission), Tom wanted to do more to evangelize the young people who were out of reach even to the Greenhouse.

The motel where Tom and his indefatigable director, Jack Fontaine, rap with 100 or so kids a night, seven nights a week, is one block off the A1A Highway. "Las Olas Boulevard and A1A is the roughest place in Fort Lauderdale," Tom says with a grin.

That is where he thinks a Jesus coffeehouse ought to be—smack amid the pimps, addicts, pushers, and prostitutes.

Every night Jack and his corps of young workers (most of them relate to the Coral Ridge church) fan out along the strip, rapping with kids and personally inviting them to His Place for coffee, punch, and cookies. A surprisingly large number drop by. Only a few openly scoff, or reject the head-on verbal witness they usually get at His Place.

There is no high-pressure hassle. Just love and concern. The small hotel lobby is usually packed out

107

with new converts, themselves the most fired up—and effective—witnesses. There is a Bible study, usually led by Tom or Jack, each night at nine. It is supposed to be over at 10—but usually is not because the kids want to keep on talking.

His Place opens at 7:30 P.M., although "beach rap" evangelism with kids on the sand, singly or in groups, may be held during the day. Often the workers take along guitars and attract a crowd with pop, rock, and Jesus music.

Jack usually locks up about 1 A.M. on weeknights, 2 or 3 A.M. on weekends. "We don't close until the kids quit coming in," advises Jack, a young bachelor with a resonant voice and instant rapport with teens.

He and a woman worker get $50 a month token pay for a forty-to-fifty hour week.

It's all worth it for just one convert like Mike, who dropped by His Place about midnight one Saturday night in mid-September. He said he planned to meet two "chicks" at the Button, a rough bar on the strip that features rock bands. A His Place worker passed Mike on the sidewalk and handed him a welcome card inviting him to the coffeehouse a block away.

The girls never showed. With nothing else to do, Mike went to His Place—and kept a date for eternity. There he met Someone else: Jesus Christ.

Tom's vision was modest enough to begin with: "If we could just speak to half a dozen kids a day, if we could lead just one to Christ, it would be tremendous!"

Ten or more decisions for Christ a week are routine; there were fifteen on one August night four months after His Place opened.

Kids who drop in may be given a copy of the "a Wayout," or "Smile, God Loves You" tract; and a copy of the Jesus newspaper, *Right On*. If they show interest, they may receive a copy of the *Reach Out New Testament*. Converts are followed up with home correspondence courses.

"We believe in working from the inside out," says Tom. "We try to get them excited about Jesus Christ and the Word of God. When you get young people into the Word, witnessing comes easily. They build up in faith and the thrill, joy, and pleasure of knowing Christ, then evangelism just happens. They just go out and do it."

The kids are better evangelists with their own kind than are the adult workers. Case in point: Sonny, a bleached-blond, long-haired youth with a pierced-ear jeweled earring in the shape of a cross.

Sonny dresses in the togs of a motorcycle club (he was a cycle gang leader before his conversion in early summer of 1971) and has the letters L-O-V-E tattooed (with a knife) on his knuckles.

Sonny goes to His Place most every night. He literally drags his friends along. One night he stomped in, two teen-age girls in tow, "bound" with the long rawhide thongs that stream from Sonny's leather wrist strap. Humorous, yes, but his way of telling them he had found something they should hear about too.

On a September Sunday morning Sonny, minus the earring and wearing a mod suit and a stubby, broad necktie, was in Coral Ridge Church. His style no doubt upset a few of the more staid parishioners, but they are gradually getting used to those like Sonny. They know that, if you scratch a hippie, you may find inside a Christian who loves Jesus more fervently than does the most conventional churchman.

Meantime, Tom and Jack are dreaming of expanding His Place to larger quarters, perhaps with space for dormitories upstairs. Kids would then have a place to "crash" for the night. There could be another type of "greenhouse" for raising new Christians.

Jim Kennedy lights up when he speaks about His Place and the Greenhouse. "It's just another illustration," he says, "of how, if you really lead people to Christ, they will find all sorts of ways to apply their faith."

14: AN IDEA WHOSE TIME HAS COME

Evangelism in Fort Lauderdale has not reached the saturation point, nor has Jim Kennedy had his fill of the Coral Ridge pastorate.

He is not seeking to move on, although he has had offers. There is too much to do right in the community where he and Anne began their ministry more than twelve years ago.

Westminster Academy just opened in the fall of 1971. The new facilities mean expanded horizons of ministry. At last the Sunday school can approach its potential enrollment.

There are vital outreach operations like Mama Bunny's Greenhouse and the beach ministry of Tom Hanna.

Jim has visions of a Bible college, seminary, and graduate school that someday may be built as part of the Coral Ridge "campus cluster."

Then, too, Jim talks about his hope of expanding the church's radio-television ministry from its present eleven stations to a world-wide outreach.

Will Jim head his own seminary someday? That is too far off for speculation now, he replies. What about teaching? "Maybe someday."

Jim feels that his temperament and disposition make him well suited to be a teacher. If it is God's plan, he might accept such a call, but not now.

To Jim, education and evangelism go together. If he

had his "druthers," though, he would settle down in some sleepy college town and teach New Testament Greek at a university or seminary.

His natural inclination, he says, is more toward teaching than evangelism: "I'm no flaming activist by temperament."

The shy, pre-Decatur Kennedy is still under the surface after all.

Once, when Jim was taking Greek studies at a continuing education seminar at Columbia Seminary, a friend pressed him: "What is it that makes you like evangelism so much?"

Jim shot back a candid—and revealing—reply: "That's not true! I really don't like it so much. I don't suppose I like it at all. If I liked it that much, I'd be studying it instead of Greek."

On the other hand, Jim can't shake the importance of evangelism—or his call to be an evangelist. He sums up its imperative grip on him in two words: "absolutely essential."

Jim does not have an inflated estimate of his importance as one of America's most successful pastors.

"I don't feel by any means that I have any more rewards than the average Christian. Don't think I have any ideas about a big pot of gold waiting for me."

Outward success is not the real yardstick of approval with God, Jim noted in a moment of introspection.

"In the overarching providence of God, He could have put me in Podunk, population 2,700. I could have had the same experience as I did in going to Decatur. I could have learned the same things, come back and taken a church of twenty-three members, and increased it to 212.

"The world would never have heard about it, but it might have been more significant than what's happening at Fort Lauderdale . . . in adjusted figures.

"Still, it would never have had the world impact."

The greatest task of the Church, according to Jim, is to fulfill the assignment given it by its General. "We cannot create any new Great Commission or any new Messiah. We have one Commission—it has not been altered. That is to take the Gospel to every creature, to make disciples of all nations, to baptize in the name of the Triune God, and to teach them to observe all things Christ has commanded us."

Doing this, he adds, not only involves evangelism and education. It also means people acting out in the physical realm the things Christ taught.

Thus, giving a cup of cold water in Christ's name or feeding the poor is part of the Great Commission.

The greatest need of the Church today, as Jim sees it, is for the laity to realize its responsibility to fulfill the Great Commission. Integral to that is the need for the clergy to realize that its task is to equip the laity—both in the classroom and through on-the-job training—to do this.

Looking ahead, Jim sees his goal: "Being used to the very greatest extent to help fulfill this need and perform this task in our generation."

This, of course, takes a variety of forms. Jim ticked off a few: the new church, Westminster Academy, the Evangelism Program, his academic work and Ph.D., and even physical fitness.

By showing to the world the most visible fruits of the Evangelism Explosion program, Jim believes he can speak to the average minister quickly.

"If he comes down to Fort Lauderdale," Jim explains, "and sees a huge and beautiful church plant that has come into existence from nothing in ten to twelve years, right away his interest is aroused."

Jim would like to see the results of the evangelism

program more attention-getting, more visible, so that still more people will become tuned in to what can be done.

"That's one reason for the whole church program, the school, and all the rest. Everything in my life is aimed at that goal."

Then as he summed up his future plans, Jim articulated some inner convictions he had never expressed before:

"The Great Commission is something that grasps the whole of one's life. This is the calling of God. This is the task of God. There is the fantastic and almost indescribable need of a world filled with eternal human beings.

"Therefore, in whatever area, in whatever way, with whatever talents, with whatever phases of my life, I feel that I have to do everything I can to make my life contribute in the greatest way possible to the fulfillment of that need. Our task is to reach billions, not thousands. Would that God would raise up men and women with this vision!"

Pursuing advanced degrees is the intellectual segment of that task, Jim believes, just as trying to stay physically fit, and using his talents, are part of the same endeavor in other realms. Everything must be bent to this task.

Erecting a building, training a staff, putting together programs, holding clinics, and producing books, films, and tapes are all part of reaching the world for Christ in this generation.

This Jim Kennedy firmly believes. Here he stands, for he can do no other.

Evangelism Explosion—and the concomitant *Kennedy Explosion*— are signs of the times. They are prominent ridges on the religious landscape of America. Because, to paraphrase Victor Hugo, the nineteenth century French poet and author, an idea whose time has come is stronger than all the armies in the world.

Dennis James Kennedy has set his sights on nothing less than reaching the entire world for Christ in this generation.

As he says: "A greater task than that, a more challenging, or a more ennobling, I cannot conceive."

A multiplying throng that has discovered the great glad news of the Gospel through the Coral Ridge approach could not agree more.

This is living with a capital "L"!

15: WHAT HAPPENS ON A VISIT

One is hard pressed to argue with the successful progress of Coral Ridge Presbyterian Church, or with the results that others who have inaugurated Dr. Kennedy's program for lay evangelism are having.

The question now, is what does all this mean to you? Could you really be as enthusiastic and successful at witnessing as all these others you have read about?

Let's look briefly at what happens to a person like you, or me, who becomes curious about the mechanics of the program.

In the chain of events that recruits you into the program you will undoubtedly come to realize that the Coral Ridge program is built on some very basic New Testament evangelism principles. The first is that every Christian has a responsibility to witness to others. This task is given to him by Jesus in the Great Commission.

Since it is your responsibility to witness, and since many Christians cannot easily explain God's purpose for sending His Son to the world, you must first be prepared to clearly explain this life-changing event to others. Your minister, or lay evangelists who have already learned how, have a responsibility to train you for ministry to others. They will be willing to help you learn.

What you must do to help them help you is agree to attend the training program and to study the recommended materials.

From the very beginning your trainer will take you with him. Oh, you'll have to talk all right! Pleasant things, like "How do you do," or "That's an interesting picture. Were you in Mexico recently?" Ice-breaker stuff. Not too much conversation, a few words to break the ice, but not enough to take the conversational lead away from the trainer. You are there for an important purpose, and your trainer needs you to be quiet and interested. Quickly he will steer the conversation into the outline he has in mind to set up the call for a Gospel presentation.

You will listen and observe.

After the call, you will probably return to the church for a talk-it-over session—and some explanations of why each point of the outline is necessary, the thinking behind it. You will learn pointers that help— where to sit, who to look at during the call. Most likely you will get an assignment too. You have an outline to learn, Scripture to memorize, illustrations to master. That's why you get four and a half months—longer if you need it—to study the program.

Weeks will pass. You will learn the materials, come to understand the philosophy and reasoning behind what you do, and continue to observe during calls.

At last the point will come in your training where you will begin to assume responsibility for parts of the presentation when you are a teammate on a call.

Then finally, one day you will solo.

Before ringing the doorbell, your team will have decided you will present the Gospel. You will be the leader and will be in charge of the conversation. You will ring the bell, and when the door is opened, you will greet the prospect, identify yourself and your church, and introduce your companions.

In all likelihood, you will be invited inside. The seating arrangement in the prospect's home is important. Your team will know this and they will seat themselves accordingly. Ideally, the prospect will be able to look at you without too much awareness of the others in the room. If there is more than one prospect, you will want to face them both rather than having to look back and forth at them.

During the introductory part of the visit your two teammates will join in the conversation. That's because the prospect will become uneasy if two people just sit there like bumps on a log.

Once you begin the approach into the Gospel, you will do all the talking. The rule for the other team members will be: "Don't speak unless spoken to." You may want to ask a team member for a testimony. He will do this keeping in mind that answers to questions not yet asked should not be given away.

Soon you will ask the first of the two key questions so vital to the presention: *"Have you come to a place in your spiritual life where you know for certain that if you were to die today you would go to Heaven?"*

That question answered, you will spring the second:

"Suppose you were to die tonight and stand before God and he were to say to you, 'Why should I let you into My Heaven' what would you say?"

You will likely be on your way into your first actual presentation of the Good News of God's plan for salvation.

Point by point you will proceed through the outline you have in mind using the illustrations you have selected and the Scripture you feel is vital to an explanation of the Gospel. You will explain about grace—that Heaven is a free gift that cannot be earned; God gives it.

You will also help your prospect understand that man is a sinner. God's justice requires Him to punish sin, but His mercy forces Him to not want to do so if He can avoid it.

God sent His Son to die for our sins. His atoning blood will cancel a sinner's wrongs if the sinner will trust Jesus for salvation.

You will lead your prospect to a commitment, and give him some material to read or study during the week.

After the Gospel has been presented, whether or not your prospect makes a decision, your entire team will again enter the conversation, making sure you leave on a friendly note. Each person will communicate his interest and concern for the prospect. After your team has gone, you want the prospect to feel that his visitors truly cared about him—not just about converting him.

After the visit is over, your team will return to the

church for refreshments and a time of sharing. See! That wasn't so bad, was it? Each team will tell what happened while it was out. A team that has just spent two hours fruitlessly driving around looking for someone at home may return rather discouraged. Your story of success will cheer them up! All teams will get an overall picture of the successes of calling and sense they have a part in the mighty work of God.

Of course evangelism doesn't end with that first call. Your program will undoubtedly include some type of follow-up procedures. You will need to make an additional call on your prospect in a week. You may also become involved in activities that integrate new converts into the life of the church.

It is practically guaranteed that once you make that first successful Gospel presentation you will be so moved by the fact that God can work through you that you will develop a consuming passion for witnessing.

To give you a preview of how simple, yet thorough the presentation outline is, we have reprinted it from *Evangelism Explosion*. Read through it to see how easy it will be for you to work with once you agree to try the program.

AN OUTLINE OF THE PRESENTATION

I. The Introduction

   A. The prospect's secular life

   B. His church background

   C. The caller's church

   D. Testimony: personal or church

   E. Two questions
      1. Have you come to the place in your spiritual life where you know for certain that if you were to die today you would go to Heaven?
      2. Suppose that you were to die tonight and stand before God and He were to say to you, "Why should I let you into My Heaven?" what would you say?

II. The Gospel

   A. Grace
      1. Heaven is a free gift (Romans 6: 23)
      2. It is not earned or deserved (Eph. 2: 8, 9)

   B. Man
      1. Is a sinner (Romans 3: 23)
      2. Cannot save himself (Titus 3: 5)

   C. God
      1. Is merciful—therefore doesn't want to punish us (I John 4: 8)
      2. Is just—therefore must punish sin (Psalm 89: 32)

D. Christ
  1. Who He is—the infinite God-man
     (John 1: 1)
  2. What He did—paid for our sins and pur-
     chased a place in Heaven for us (Isaiah 53:
     4) which He offers as a gift that may be
     received by . . . .

E. Faith
  1. What it is not—mere intellectual assent
     nor temporal faith (James 2: 19)
  2. What it is—trusting in Jesus Christ alone
     for salvation (Acts 16: 31)

III. The Commitment

  A. The qualifying question:
     Does that make sense to you?

  B. The commitment question:
     Do you want to receive the gift of eternal life?

  C. The clarification of commitment:
     Would you like to transfer your trust, that is,
     your hope of getting into Heaven . . . from
     yourself and what you have been doing, to what
     Christ has done for you?

  D. The prayer of commitment (Matthew 18: 20)

  E. The assurance of salvation (John 6: 47)

Adapted from Evangelism Explosion, © 1970 by D. James Kennedy. Published by Tyndale House Publishers, Wheaton, Illinois. Used by permission.

In the course of your training, you will have all the points of the outline explained to you. Your leader will help you find Scripture and illustrations to use to explain the Gospel to others in terms that are clear to you and them. You will not be likely to find yourself in a position of not knowing what to say next. Neither will you have such a memorized speech that you dare not depart from it. The feature that makes lay evangelists like yourself so successful is that suddenly you come to such a clear understanding of God's plan and your assurance that you are able to give to anyone who asks, in any way, a reason for the hope you hold. The thought of witnessing will no longer fill you with fear and trembling because it won't be a big unknown. Fear will be replaced with confidence—and satisfaction at doing what Jesus commanded. *Soli Deo Gloria.*

BIBLIOGRAPHY

Autrey, C. E. 1964. *Evangelism in the Acts*. Grand Rapids: Zondervan Publishing House.

Chafin, K. 1966. *Help! I'm a Layman*. Waco, Texas: Word Books, Inc.

Coleman, R. E. 1969. *Dry Bones Can Live Again*. Old Tappan, New Jersey: Fleming H. Revell Company.

Coleman, R. E. 1968. *The Master Plan of Evangelism*. Old Tappan, New Jersey: Fleming H. Revell Company.

Kennedy, D. J. 1970. *Evangelism Explosion*. Wheaton, Illinois: Tyndale House Publishers.

Kettner, E. A. 1964. *Adventures in Evangelism*. St. Louis: Concordia.

Little, P. E. 1966. *How to Give Away Your Faith*. Downers Grove, Illinois: Inter-Varsity Press.

Lockyer, H. 1954. *The Art of Winning Souls*. Grand Rapids: Zondervan Publishing House.

Lowry, O. 1962. *Scripture Memorizing for Successful Soul-Winning*. Grand Rapids: Zondervan Publishing House.

McDormand, T. B. 1969. *The Christian Must Have the Answer*. Nashville: Broadman Press.

Rinker, R. 1962. *You Can Witness with Confidence*. Grand Rapids: Zondervan Publishing House.

Stott, J. R. 1969. *Our Guilty Silence*. Grand Rapids: Eerdmans.

Two "Kennedy Books" concerned laymen should know about

over 100,000 in print
EVANGELISM EXPLOSION

by D. James Kennedy

The how-to-do-it for people who want to study the Coral Ridge method in depth. Contains a sample presentation, illustrations, Scripture notations, and a discourse on the philosophies of the program.
Publisher: Tyndale House

The story behind the man
THE KENNEDY EXPLOSION

by E. Russell Chandler

Laymen are excited over what's happening to them personally. Coral Ridge Presbyterian Church and others, here and abroad, are growing in an age of declining church attendance. Why? This book tells the story.
Publisher: David C. Cook Publishing Co.

The Evangelism Program
on TAPE and FILM

KENNEDY CASSETTES
on Lay Evangelism

On four 60-minute tapes, Dr. D. James Kennedy, direct from the Coral Ridge Clinic on Evangelism, explains—in his own words—in his warm, lively way—what the program is and how to use his outline and method.
Producer: David C. Cook Publishing Co.

LIKE A MIGHTY ARMY and TEACHER-TRAINING FILMS—The D. James Kennedy Program

The dramatic story of Dr. D. James Kennedy and the Coral Ridge Church growth will inspire your congregation to use the training films—a condensed evangelism clinic similar to the one at Coral Ridge.
Producer: Gospel Films Production

Order these items from your local Christian bookstore or write David C. Cook Publishing Co., Elgin, IL 60120 for information.